# A PLANE VIEW OF THE BIBLE

An Overview of the Bible
In 10 Historical Periods

*G. Michael Cocoris*

© 2010, 2025 G. Michael Cocoris

All rights reserved. This publication may not be reproduced (in whole or in part, edited, or revised) in any way, form, or means, including, but not limited to electronic, mechanical, photocopying, recording or any kind of storage and retrieval system *for sale*, except for brief quotations in printed reviews, without the written permission of G. Michael Cocoris, 2016 Euclid #20, Santa Monica, CA 90405, michaelcocoris@gmail.com, or his appointed representatives. Permission is hereby granted, however, for reproduction of the whole or parts of the whole without changing the content in any way for *free distribution,* provided all copies contain this copyright notice in its entirety. Permission is also granted to charge for the cost of copying.

Unless otherwise indicated, all Scripture quotations are taken from the New King James Version ®, Copyright © 1979, 1980, 1982 by Thomas Nelson, Inc. Used by permission. All rights reserved.

Cover design by John Cocoris

Interior design by John Cocori

# TABLE OF CONTENTS

| | | |
|---|---|---|
| Preface | | |
| Introduction | | 1 |
| Chapter 1 | The Patriarchs | 11 |
| | The Patriarchal Family | 24 |
| Chapter 2 | The Exodus | 25 |
| | The Tabernacle | 37 |
| | The Offerings | 41 |
| | The Festivals | 45 |
| Chapter 3 | The Conquest | 51 |
| Chapter 4 | The Judges | 63 |
| Chapter 5 | The United Kingdom | 69 |
| Chapter 6 | The Divided Kingdom | 77 |
| | The Chronology of The Divided Kingdom | 95 |
| | The Spirituality of The Kings | 97 |
| Chapter 7 | The Captivity | 99 |
| Chapter 8 | The Restoration | 103 |
| | Between The Testaments | 109 |
| Chapter 9 | The Ministry of Christ | 113 |
| Chapter 10 | The Acts of the Apostles | 125 |
| Conclusion | | 133 |

# TABLE OF CONTENTS

**Appendix**                                               **135**

    **Mesopotamia**
    **Egypt**
    **Assyria**
    **Babylonia**
    **Persia**
    **Rome**

**About The Author**                            **157**

# PREFACE

In the late 1950s, as a freshman in college, I was required to take a Bible Survey course. The professor began by dictating thirteen periods of Bible History. There were no copy machines in those days, and professors did not use mimeographed material. A fellow student somehow discovered that the professor was following a small book of less than a hundred pages entitled *Outlines of Bible History* by P. E. Burroughs. The Sunday School Board of the Southern Baptist Convention originally published it in 1934. Once we discovered his "secret," we bought the book. Then, instead of taking notes, we sat in class following the professor as he lectured almost point for point through the book.

In my first year in seminary, another professor did something similar. He, too, outlined twelve or thirteen periods of Bible History. I found these periods of Bible History to be immensely beneficial for grasping an overview of the whole of Scripture.

After graduating from seminary, I directed several tours to Israel. The guides in Israel covered so much material that people on the tour often got lost in the details. I discovered that telling them about those "periods of Bible History" helped them understand the tour guides better but also helped them comprehend a synopsis of the Bible, in many cases, for the first time.

I acknowledge my indebtedness to those who have instructed me in the periods of Bible History. I am particularly indebted to

*Preface*

that small volume entitled *Outlines of Bible History*. Those professors and that book got me started, but I have reduced the periods to ten, revised the explanations, changed a number of the dates, and added material.

I also deeply appreciate several people who helped me with this project. Leonard Wilson typed the manuscript. Gladys Watchulonis originally proofread it, and Teresa Rogers proofread the revision. David Drummond gave me very valuable suggestions.

May the Lord use this presentation to give you a better understanding of His Word and, more importantly, a closer relationship with Him.

G. Michael Cocoris
Santa Monica, California

# INTRODUCTION

The Bible is a big book. Look at its size. It is a library containing 66 books, comprising 1,189 chapters (929 in the Old Testament and 260 in the New Testament). Think about that. Most of the books we read have only a handful of chapters. The Bible has 1,189 chapters. That is a big book!

Consider the content of the Bible. Hundreds of characters parade across its pages from the beginning of human existence to about AD 95. (It was written over approximately 1500 years.) While most of the events of the Bible took place in Palestine, not all were in the same location. Hundreds of places, including mountains, valleys, bodies of water, nations, cities, and towns, appear on the pages of Scripture. Moreover, the people in the Bible had a variety of customs. The Bible is indeed a big book.

How is it possible to grasp so much material? Getting a grasp of the Bible is like getting an overview of a large city. Many years ago, a college buddy took me up in a small plane and gave me the layout of Houston, Texas. He began by pointing out the main freeways that divide the city into sections. Then he showed me things in the sections, like the Astrodome. Likewise, a "plane view" of the Bible will make it plain.

# A Plane View of The Bible

A simple way to get a plane view or overview of the Bible is by becoming aware of its time frames or "historical periods." These *periods* usually contain one or two (sometimes more) main *characters* who lived at different *times* in various *places* and practiced various *customs*. So, to gain a basic grasp of the Bible, begin with its historical periods, identify the main characters, note the dates, and notice where they were, what they did, and how they did things. This is the "who, what, when, where, and how" of the Bible. The historical periods of the Bible contain the "who" and "what." Chronology indicates "when." The geography of the Bible focuses on "where," and the customs of the Bible reveal "how" people did things.

## The Historical Periods

The Scripture can be divided into ten historical periods. These time frames are not debatable. Though scholars may debate the dates, all theologians from every theological perspective would agree that the ten periods of Bible history are accurate.

What are the ten historical periods in the Bible? To answer that question, it is necessary first to isolate the historical material in the Bible. The Old Testament can be divided into four parts. The Pentateuch consists of five books from Genesis to Deuteronomy. The twelve historical books extend from Joshua to Esther. Then follow five poetical books: Job, Psalms, Proverbs, Ecclesiastes, and the Song of Solomon. The fourth and final division of the Old Testament is the prophetical books, consisting of seventeen books

*Introduction*

from Isaiah to Malachi. The prophetic books are divided into the Major and Minor Prophets.

Likewise, the New Testament can be divided into four parts. The first four books, Matthew through John, consist of Gospels. The book of Acts is the lone historical book. Then follows twenty-one epistles beginning with Romans and ending with Jude. These are often divided into Pauline and general epistles. The final type of book in the New Testament and the last book in the Bible is a prophetical book called Revelation.

This simple survey quickly reveals that only some of the books of the Bible are "historical." The books designated historical are books of history, but so are some of the books in the Pentateuch and the Gospels. Therefore, to read the *history* in the Bible, one need only read Genesis, Exodus, Numbers, Deuteronomy, Joshua, Judges, 1 and 2 Samuel, 1 and 2 Kings, Ezra, Nehemiah, Mark (or Matthew or Luke), and Acts.

Those sixteen books cover all of the history in the Bible. To read the Bible through *historically*, you do not have to read sixty-six books, only sixteen! That is a version of a condensed Bible. All the other books of the Bible fit within the historical framework of those sixteen books.

To put the same thing another way, the Old and New Testaments are laid out in such a fashion that first, the historical material is given and then other material is added. In the Old Testament, the poetry and prophecy written during that historical period are added after the historical period. In the New Testament, the letters and prophecy of the period are added after the historical period.

## A Plane View of The Bible

Let me illustrate. I was born in 1939. I graduated from high school in 1958, college in 1962, and seminary in 1966. After I graduated from seminary, I was an itinerate evangelist from 1966 to 1979. In 1979, I became the pastor of a church. Now, let me tell you about a poem that I wrote while I was in college. Let me share a letter I wrote while I was in seminary. Here is a sermon I preached as an evangelist and one I delivered as a pastor. In other words, after I gave you a historical overview of my life, I mentioned a poem, a letter, and a sermon I preached *during* those various periods. In a similar fashion, both the Old and New Testaments first give us the historical layout. Then follow poetry, prophecy, and letters written *during* those historical periods.

From the historical material in the Bible, ten historical periods emerge.

| | | |
|---|---|---|
| Origins | Genesis 1-11 | |
| 1. The Patriarchs | Genesis 12-50 | 2167-1860 BC |
| 2. The Exodus | Exodus-Deuteronomy | 1527-1407 BC |
| 3. The Conquest | Joshua | 1407-1400 BC |
| 4. The Judges | Judges–I Samuel 8 | 1375-1043 BC |
| 5. The United Kingdom | 1 Samuel 9:1-1 Kings 11:43 | 1043-931 BC |
| 6. The Divided Kingdom | 1 Kings 12:1-2 Kings 16 | 931-605 BC |
| 7. The Captivity | 2 Kings 17-25 | 605-536 BC |
| 8. The Restoration | Ezra-Esther | 536-400 BC |
| 9. The Ministry of Christ | Matthew-John | 6/5 BC-AD 30 |
| 10. The Acts of the Apostles | Acts | AD 30-95 |

*Introduction*

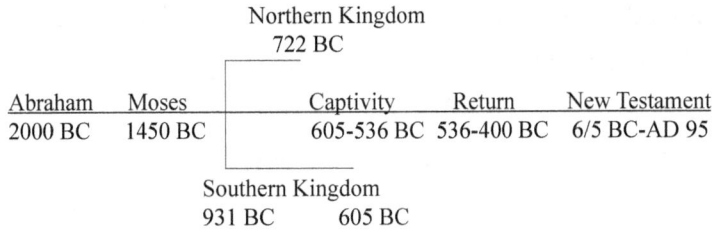

Is the "history" in the Bible historical? Are the places mentioned in the Bible authentic locations? Are the people actual human beings? Are the events factual episodes? Are dates in the Bible accurate? In short, is the Bible true history, or is it a myth?

For those who believe that the Bible is the Word of God, if the Bible says it happened, it actually happened. After all, if God inspired it, since He cannot lie (Titus 1:2), it cannot contain falsehood. Thus, the record is assumed to be true and without error.

Needless to say, not everyone accepts that. Some want proof outside the Bible. Is there evidence apart from the Bible that it contains history? Yes. Many archaeological discoveries have verified the accuracy of the record, including places, people, and events. Not every place, person, or event can be proven historical by archaeology. Furthermore, archaeologists debate among themselves whether or not some of the discoveries confirm an account. Nevertheless, archaeology has repeatedly demonstrated the historical accuracy of the Scripture and *not one unquestioned archaeological discovery has proven that the Bible is in error at any point.* It is reasonable to assume that if so much has been proven historical, the remainder is also. At least, it is reasonable to conclude that since so much of the Bible has been proven historically accurate, the rest could be.

## Chronology

If the Bible's people, places, and events are historical, there is a time frame and a chronology. Chronology is the arrangement of events in time, which necessitates determining the sequence of events and establishing specific dates.

Biblical chronology is complex. In ancient times, there was no single, universally recognized dating system. Time was not divided into BC and AD until hundreds of years after Christ. Among the ancients, not even the year and months were the same. Furthermore, some of the chronological details within the Scripture seem to disagree with each other, especially in the books of Judges, 1 Kings, and 2 Kings. Then, there is the problem of correlating the chronology of the Bible with the chronology of other nations with whom Israel came in contact. All of these problems have been solved.

A standard dating system has been established. In AD 525, Dionysius Exiguus divided history into BC and AD. Since then, the year has been standardized on a solar year, and all calendars have been adjusted.

Several factors make definite data dating possible. The problems of chronology within the Bible (Judges and Kings) have been solved (see Edwin Thiele, *The Mysterious Numbers of the Hebrew Kings*). Archaeologists have discovered Assyrian records

## Introduction

containing a list of all Assyrian years and astronomical information, such as an eclipse of the sun. The astronomical data makes it possible to determine specific dates in Assyrian history. With one Assyrian date fixed absolutely, every other year in Assyrian history can be identified. It is now generally agreed that the exact dates for the significant Assyrian rulers during the first millennium BC are known.

Since some events are recorded in both and secular history and the date for the secular event can be firmly fixed, the dates for figures as far back as the death of Solomon in 931 BC are also certain.

Unfortunately, dates for the second millennium BC cannot yet be correlated. Therefore, before 931 BC, all dating must be computed within the Scripture. Because there are gaps in the genealogies of the early chapters of Genesis and because there is no conclusive evidence that Nahor was the actual father of Terah (He could have been the grandfather, etc.), the earliest specific date that can be determined based on chronology is the birth of Terah, the father of Abraham, in 2295 BC.

## Geography

The land of Palestine, the land stage on which most of the events of the Bible took place, is about the size of the state of New Jersey. It extends from Dan in the north to Beersheba in the south, a distance of 150 miles. On the west is the Mediterranean Sea; on the east are the Sea of Galilee, the Jordan River, and the Dead Sea.

The width varies. The northern portion is only about 30 miles wide, while the southern part is about 90 miles wide. A mountainous region runs down the center of the land. Thus, there is a coastal plain between the Mediterranean Sea and the mountains and a valley between the mountains and the Sea of Galilee, the Jordan River, and the Dead Sea.

The Sea of Galilee is a beautiful body of water about nine by twelve miles. It empties into the Jordan River, which meanders southward toward the Dead Sea. As the crow flies, the distance between the Sea of Galilee and the Dead Sea is approximately 60 miles, but because the Jordan River twists and turns so much, the same trip in a canoe would cover 120 miles. The Jordan River flows into the Dead Sea, thirteen hundred feet below sea level, making it the lowest point on the earth's surface. It is also 33% salt. Therefore, nothing can live in it.

## Customs

The Bible is full of customs. A custom may be defined as a common practice among a group of people. It is usually a long-established practice that is considered an unwritten law. These repeated practices or conventions regulate social life.

One of the difficulties in understanding parts of the Bible is that some of the customs practiced by the people in it are foreign to our culture. We live in houses; they lived in tents. We wear a robe after we get out of the shower and before we put on our clothes. In ancient times, robe-like garments were their clothes.

## Introduction

Imagine men in skirts! We ride in cars, buses, trains, and planes. They rode on animals or in chariots. This is only a small sample of our culture and customs differences. To complicate matters, some customs remained the same throughout history and others changed. There are cases where a particular custom was practiced in only one period.

**Summary:** The Bible is a big book, but like getting the layout of a large city by flying over it in a plane, it is also possible to get the "big picture" of the Bible by looking at its historical periods and the people, places, and practices within them.

The main focus of what follows is the ten historical periods and the main figures and events. That is the key to getting a bird's eye view of the Bible. The discussion of these periods is seasoned with references to archaeology, chronology, geography, and, in a few cases, customs. The Bible mentions thousands of places and customs. The sheer volume of material prohibits a discussion of each one. For additional information, consult a Bible dictionary, a Bible atlas, or a book on Bible customs.

In some cases, additional important material about the period, like a discussion of the Tabernacle, is added after the chapter on that period. Also, during the historical periods of the Bible, other nations rose and fell. The appendix briefly explains the nations that came in contact with Israel. It is not necessary to read that material to get an overview of the Bible, but it is interesting and sometimes helpful information.

## A Plane View of The Bible

One other word. The Bible contains history, but it is not a history book. Its history can be verified by archaeology, and its chronology can be confirmed by archaeology and astronomy, but that is not the point. In the final analysis, the Bible was written to teach spiritual truth, that is, to give people knowledge of salvation (2 Tim. 3:15) and to assist believers in growth to spiritual maturity (2 Tim. 3:16-17). Just understanding Bible history, chronology, geography, and customs will not, of course, accomplish any of that. Spiritual birth is by faith (Jn. 3:3, 16), and spiritual growth comes through faith, loving obedience, etc. (see *How To Live A Biblical Spiritual Life*, by this author). The ten periods of Bible history will only enable us to understand the Bible's layout. That, however, is helpful. It allows us to find our way around the Bible to absorb its spiritual truth.

Chapter 1

# THE PATRIARCHS

The Bible does not begin with the period of the Patriarchs. First, there are eleven chapters in Genesis, which are a fitting introduction to the whole Bible. These opening chapters could be entitled "Origins" because they give the origin of 1) **The universe** (Gen. 1). The Bible opens with the declaration that "In the beginning, God created the heavens and the earth" (Gen. 1:1). The remainder of Genesis 1 describes how God formed and filled the earth, climaxing with the creation of humans. 2) **Humans** (Gen. 2). God created humans from the dust of the ground and breathed into them the breath of life. God placed Adam and Eve in the Garden of Eden. 3) **Sin** (Gen. 3-4). God told Adam and Eve they could eat of every tree of the Garden of Eden except the tree of the knowledge of good and evil. In the form of a serpent, Satan tempted Eve, who took the fruit and gave it to Adam. Thus, sin entered the scene. 4) **The present state** (Gen. 6-9). As a result of great wickedness, God sent judgment on the earth in the form of a flood. As a result, conditions such as rain exist today. 5) **Languages** (Gen. 11). When men tried to reach heaven by building a tower, God confused them by giving them different languages. Thus, in the opening chapters of Genesis, God created the earth and man.

Sin entered, producing violence (Gen. 4), judgment (Gen. 6-9), and division (Gen. 11).

The period of the Patriarchs begins in Genesis 12. Technically, this period should begin with the birth of Abraham (2167 BC) and end with the death of the last patriarch, Jacob (1860 BC). However, the book of Genesis includes the life of Joseph, who died in 1806 BC. So, the period of the Patriarchs extends from 2167 BC to 1806 BC.

## Abraham

Abram (Gen. 11:27-25:11), later named Abraham, lived from 2167 BC to 1992 BC. His story revolves around two issues: *a land* (Palestine) God promised to give him and his descendants, and *a son* God promised to give him from whom would come not only a great nation but also a blessing to the world.

*From Ur to Canaan (Gen. 11:27-12:9)* Abram lived in Ur of the Chaldees, a city in southern Mesopotamia 220 miles south of modern Baghdad in Iraq. Ur gradually disappeared from history after about the sixth century BC because of a change in the Euphrates River that left the area without an adequate water supply for irrigation.

The site of the ancient city was unknown until J. E. Taylor identified it in 1854. Since then, it has been excavated extensively. The wall around the city was 2½ miles in circumference and 77 feet thick. Sir Leonard Woolley, one of the archaeologists who excavated Ur (1922-34), estimated the city's population and its

## The Patriarchs

suburbs to be about 250,000.

When Abram lived in Ur, it was at its height. It was a highly civilized (by this time, the pyramids of Egypt had been built!) and prosperous city. Woolley said that the architects of Ur were "familiar with all the basic principles of construction known to us today." Houses had ten to twenty rooms, and, in some cases, the guestroom was adjoined by a lavatory. Education included reading, writing, mathematics, multiplication and division tables, square cube roots, and practical geometry. Merchants conducted business and recorded their transactions in writing.

Archeologists have also discovered Ur had great temples, commercial activity, and literary works. Tax records, letters of credit, court cases, invoices, artistic vessels, and beautiful jewelry have been unearthed. For example, at one gravesite, they found inlaid harps and two statues of goats standing erect before a bush and, in another, a helmet fashioned from solid gold in the form of a wig with locks of hair hammered in relief and engraved in a delicate symmetrical form.

At least once, Terah, Abram's father, was an idolater (Josh. 24:2). Archaeologists have discovered that Ur was an idolatrous and immoral city. In 1922, Woolley excavated a ziggurat built during the Third Dynasty of Ur (*ca.* 2060-1950 BC). A ziggurat is a tower in the form of a terraced pyramid, with each story smaller than the one below it (like the layers of a wedding cake) and a temple on top. The ziggurat found at Ur was two hundred feet long, one hundred fifty feet in width, and seventy feet in height. Excavations indicate that the worship of the Moon-god Nannar prevailed there. While living in Ur, the Lord appeared to Abram and instructed him to: "Get out of your country, from your family and from your father's house, to a land that I will show you. I will make you a great nation; I will bless you and make your name great; and you shall be a blessing. I will bless those who bless you, and I will curse him who curses you, and in you all the families of the earth shall be blessed" (Gen. 12:1-3; see Acts 7:2-3).

This is the seed plot of the Bible. God promised Abram land and descendants, who would not only occupy the land but would also bless the world. The Old Testament is the story of God giving the land of Palestine to Abram's descendants, the Jews, and the New Testament is the record of God sending His Son Jesus Christ, who is of Jewish descent, to the world so that the world might be blessed.

Abram and some of his relatives moved about 600 miles from Ur to Haran. Haran has been continuously occupied since the third millennium BC. It is in southern Turkey. Apart from the Bible, written materials from this time frequently refer to Haran. In fact, either from literary or archaeological evidence, virtually all of the towns mentioned in connection with the Patriarchs have been shown to date back to the time of the Patriarchs, including Shechem, Bethel, Jericho, Salem, Gerar, Dothan, and Beersheba. Also, names such as Abram, Isaac, Jacob, Laban, and Joseph are common by the beginning of the second millennium BC.

The city of Mari is not mentioned in the Bible. It was on the trade route between Ur and Haran. In 1933, while excavating Mari, French archaeologist Andre Parrot discovered a large number of letters, including administrative records and correspondence. The Mari texts and the tablets of Nuzu (another city in the area) reveal that the customs of the Patriarchs recorded in Genesis were common during the time in which Genesis says they lived.

Thus, scholars have concluded that the patriarchal accounts in Genesis reflect the early second millennium BC. As the famous American archaeologist W. F. Albright has pointed out, the Patriarchs had the same names, visited the same places, and practiced the same customs as their contemporaries.

The family remained in Haran until Abram's father died. Abram then moved to Canaan. Once in Canaan, he erected an altar and worshipped the Lord at Shechem.

*To Egypt and back (Gen. 12:10-20)* When famine came to Canaan, Abram journeyed to Egypt. He returned with great wealth and lived temporarily at Bethel. These early episodes pertain to getting Abram to the land of promise and keeping him there.

*Separation from and rescue of Lot (Gen. 13:1-14:24; 18:1-19:38)* God had told Abram to "leave his father's house," but Abram took Lot, his nephew. Perhaps he did this because, not having a son, his nephew was in line to be his heir, but God intended to give Abram a biological son to be his heir. The separation from Lot did not come early or all at once.

A conflict developed between the herdsmen of Abram and those of Lot. Abram let Lot choose the part of the land he wished. Lot chose the richest part, the well-watered plains of Jericho. Abram journeyed to the hill country. At this point, God appeared to him again and told him to look as far as he could to the north, east, south, and west. It was all of that land that God promised to him (Gen. 13:14-17). However, Abram's dealings with Lot were not finished. Abram had to rescue Lot twice, once from the eastern kings (Gen. 14:1-24) and once at Sodom and Gomorrah (Gen. 18:1-19:29).

*The Covenant with Abram (Gen. 15:1-21)* God told Abram that his descendants would be as numerous as the stars he could see (Gen. 15:2-5). Abram "believed in the Lord, and He accounted it to him for righteousness" (Gen. 15:6). When Abram asked how he would know this would happen, God made a covenant with him that included giving Abram's descendants the land from the river of Egypt to great river, the River Euphrates (Gen. 15:9-21).

There are two very important issues here. First, Abram was declared righteous not by doing something but by simply believing, that is, trusting in the Lord. This is the teaching of justification by faith, which is when a person trusts Jesus Christ for eternal life, that individual is not only declared "not guilty" but also "righteous" in the sight of God. God does this not because He overlooks the sin of which people are guilty but because Jesus Christ died to pay the penalty of sin. The New Testament quotes Genesis 15:6 to support this vital teaching (Rom. 4:3; Gal. 3:6; Jas. 2:23).

Thus, the teaching of justification by faith is not just a New Testament concept; it is an Old Testament idea that appears in the very first book of the Bible. When the Judaizers of Paul's day wanted to go back to the Law of Moses to argue that a person had to keep the Law of Moses to be justified, Paul countered with, in essence, "You didn't go back far enough. You want to go back to Exodus, but you need to go to Genesis. If you do that, you will soon discover that justification is by faith, not by works" (Gal. 3). Justification by faith is one of the most important spiritual truths in the Bible.

The second issue is that God made an unconditional blood covenant with Abram to give his descendants the land. In other words, God put His promise in a contract.

In ancient times, there were different types of covenants. Though not specifically mentioned during the period of the Patriarchs, a shoe covenant existed in ancient times. Ruth 4:7 says, "Now this was the custom in former times in Israel concerning redeeming and exchanging to confirm anything; one man took off his sandal and gave it to the other and this was an attestation in Israel." The shoe covenant was the least binding of all types of covenants. It simply said that the covenant was binding as long as one possessed the shoe or sandal of another.

Again, though not specifically mentioned during the period of the Patriarchs, the Bible speaks of a "covenant of salt" (Num. 18:19; 2 Chron. 13:5). People in ancient times carried a pouch of salt with them at all times. When entering into a covenant with each other, the two would take pinches of salt from each other's bag and put it in their own, the idea being that the covenant was binding until those granules of salt were returned to their original owner. That would have been impossible. Thus, the covenant was irrevocable.

## A Plane View of The Bible

In Genesis 15, God made a covenant with Abram. He did not swap shoes or grains of salt with him. Instead, He established a blood covenant. The Lord told Abram to bring him a three-year-old heifer, a three-year-old female goat, a three-year-old ram, a turtledove, and a young pigeon. Abram was to cut the animals (but not the birds) in half and place each half opposite the other. Then, while Abram was asleep, "a smoking oven and a burning torch" passed through the pieces (Gen. 15:9-21). The fire was an indication of the Divine Presence. In ancient times, the significance of the blood covenant was that it was an eternal, irrevocable covenant. The idea was that the covenant was binding until the blood once again flowed in the veins of the animals from which it came. Since that was impossible, the covenant was thought to be irrevocable. Thus, God made a blood covenant, an eternal, irrevocable covenant, with Abram and his seed to give them the land of Palestine. In the same way, the blood of Christ, a blood covenant that is eternal and irrevocable, redeems believers.

*The Son of Hagar (Gen. 16:1-16)* God made a covenant to give Abram's descendants Palestine. That necessitated a son, but Abram was old and his wife was past childbearing age. So Sarah suggested that Abram have a son by her handmaiden, Hagar.

Her proposal was in accord with the prevailing custom in northern Mesopotamia. Nuzu was an ancient city east of the Tigris River. Between 1925-31, during the excavation of Nuzu, more than twenty thousand clay tablets were found, including administrative records, business records, lawsuits, marriage contracts, private correspondence, wills, etc. The marriage contract stated that if the wife was barren, she could provide a slave girl for her husband, which is what Sarah did (Gen. 16:1-2).

Abram's son by Hagar was named Ishmael. Ishmael was not the son God promised nor the one to fulfill God's covenant. The world has never recovered from Abram's one night in the tent with Hagar. Ishmael's descendants became the Arab nations. Today, they are the great opponents of Israel.

*The Seal of the Covenant (Gen. 17:1-27)* Again, God appeared to Abram, changing his name from Abram, which means "exalted father," to Abraham, which means "father of a multitude." God also gave him circumcision as a sign of the covenant.

*The Son of Promise (Gen. 21:1-23:20)* God had promised Abraham a son and God gave him a son, Isaac, from the womb of his wife Sarah, even though Abraham was 100 years old at the time (Gen. 21:1-7).

Years later, God appeared to Abraham with a surprising and startling command: "Take now your son, your only son Isaac, whom you love, and go up to the land of Moriah and offer him there as a burnt offering on one of the mountains which I shall tell you" (Gen. 22:2). In believing obedience, Abraham took Isaac, along with firewood for an altar, and traveled three days to Mt. Moriah. Isaac was spared when God provided a sacrifice. The book of Hebrews tells us that Abraham did this by faith (Heb. 11:17-19). Isaac was a willing participant who also trusted God.

Eventually, Sarah, the mother of the son of promise, died (Gen. 23). After Isaac's marriage (Gen. 24), Abraham also died (Gen. 25:7-11).

## Isaac

After the death of Abraham, Genesis records a brief history of his son Ishmael (Gen. 25:12-18) and then focuses on his son Isaac (Gen. 25:19-26), who lived from 2067 BC to 1887 BC. The stories of Abraham and Isaac overlap. After all, they were father and son. While living with his father, he was offered to the Lord and he was married.

*The Marriage of Isaac (Gen. 24:1-67)* When Isaac was forty years old, Abraham sent a servant to Haran to bring back a wife for his son. Rebekah, the daughter of Abraham's brother, was selected. She left her family and homeland to be Isaac's wife.

The customs surrounding getting married during this period differed from those of later times in the Bible and, of course, from today's. Their marriage custom that strikes us as the most strange is their method of choosing a wife. The bridegroom did not choose his own bride. Instead, the couple's parents negotiated the transaction and the young people were expected to acquiesce to the arrangement. Hagar chose a wife for Ishmael (Gen. 21:21). Abraham sent a trusted servant hundreds of miles to select a wife for his son, whom his son had never seen (Gen. 24:1-4). Isaac gave Jacob instructions in this custom (Gen. 28:1). Judah selected a wife for Er (Gen. 38:6). If a young man violated this custom and chose a wife on his own, he caused great grief for his parents (Gen. 26:35, 27:46). However, the son did have the privilege of suggesting his personal preference to his parents, as did Shechem (Gen. 34:4).

## The Patriarchs

Why did the parents reserve the right to select a bride for their son? Perhaps, since the bride was to become a member of the clan, the whole family was interested in knowing if she would be suitable. Abraham stated that he sent his servant so far away for a wife for Isaac because he did not want him to marry a Canaanite (Gen. 24:3).

Modern Westerners have difficulty with this system because we believe that love should come before and be the basis of marriage. The ancient Oriental idea was that people were to love the individuals they married. There are indications of that in the Scriptures, for the Bible tells us that when Isaac and Rebekah were married, they had never seen each other. Yet, it says, "Then Isaac brought her into his mother Sarah's tent and took Rebekah and she became his wife and he loved her" (Gen. 24:67). The Bible also gives examples of cases of love before marriage. With Jacob and Rachel, it was love at first sight (Gen. 29:10-18). It was genuine love that lasted, for he labored fourteen years before he could take her as his wife (Gen. 29:20). There are other examples of love before marriage in the Scripture (Judges 14:2; 1 Sam. 18:20).

*The Sons of Isaac (Gen. 25:19-34)* Isaac and Rebekah had twin sons, Esau and Jacob. As the oldest, Esau was in line to receive the family inheritance. Jacob, however, bought the birthright from Esau. According to the tablets of Nuzu, it was legitimate for a birthright to be negotiated. One tablet records the transfer of inheritance rights to an adopted brother, and another records a man selling his birthright for three sheep.

*The Covenant with Isaac (Gen. 26:23-25)* God reaffirmed with Isaac the covenant made with Abraham (see also Gen. 17:19, 21).

## Jacob

Although Isaac had not yet died, Genesis turns the spotlight on Jacob (Gen. 27-50), who lived from 2007 BC to 1860 BC.

*The Blessing of Isaac (Gen. 27:1-40)* Having bargained with Esau and being directed by Rebekah, his mother, Jacob deceived his father Isaac into giving him the blessing. According to records discovered at Nuzu, deathbed pronouncements constituted a person's last will and testament and were regarded as legally binding and irrevocable. Again, the practices of the Patriarchs reflect Mesopotamia of the second millennium BC.

*The Flight to Haran (Gen. 27:41-28:9)* To avoid Esau's wrath and find a wife from among his mother's people, Jacob fled to Haran.

*The Covenant with Jacob (Gen. 28:10-22)* On the way out of the land, Jacob had a dream in which God reaffirmed to him the covenant made with Abraham.

*The Marriage of Jacob (Gen. 29:1-30:43)* For the privilege of marrying Rachel, Jacob served her father, Laban, for seven years. The deceiver, however, was deceived and ended up with Rachel's sister, Leah. So Jacob served another seven years to marry Rachel. After that, he worked six more years and, in so doing, increased his wealth considerably.

# The Patriarchs

*Return to Canaan (Gen. 31:1-35:29).* Because of differences with his father-in-law, Jacob eventually fled from Haran. Laban overtook him, and the two reconciled. Jacob then continued to Shechem, where Abraham had first built an altar. Jacob had twelve sons. Those sons became the heads of the twelve tribes of Israel.

*Journey to Egypt (Gen. 37:1-50:26)* Of his twelve sons, Jacob's favorite was Joseph (1916-1806 BC). Consequently, Joseph's jealous brothers hated him and sold him into slavery. In the providence of God, Joseph ended up in a high position in Egypt. Because of a famine, Jacob and his entire household also ended up in Egypt. Under the protection of his son Joseph, the last patriarch spent the last seventeen years of his life in Egypt.

There are only three Patriarchs: Abraham, Isaac, and Jacob. From looking at the material given to each of them in the book of Genesis, it would appear that one of the sons of the third patriarch, Joseph, is given an inordinate amount of space. His story covers Genesis 37-50. The reason for this is that one of the purposes of writing Genesis is to explain to the children of Israel how they ended up in Egypt. To do that, Moses had to elaborate on the events in Joseph's life.

**Summary**: During the period of the Patriarchs, God called Abraham in Ur of the Chaldees and promised to give him land and to make him a great nation. Abraham journeyed to Canaan and had a son named Isaac. Isaac had a son named Jacob, who had twelve sons who became the twelve tribes of Israel, but they all ended up in Egypt. The fulfillment of God's promise for a land

and a great nation was delayed.

During this period, Mesopotamia was the center of civilization. See the appendix for a brief overview of the history of Mesopotamia.

The single most significant fact of this period is that *God promised the land to the Patriarchs.* Each of the three Patriarchs, Abraham (Gen. 15:18-21), Isaac (Gen. 26:1-5), and Jacob (Gen. 28:13-15) was given a promise by God of the land.

The great spiritual truth of this period is that people are justified (that is, declared righteous) by faith (Gen. 15:6).

### The Patriarchal Family

The Patriarchal family can be confusing. Who was married to whom? To complicate matters, one Patriarch had two wives. All three had more than one son. Which son was in line for the inheritance? It was not always the firstborn, as was the custom.

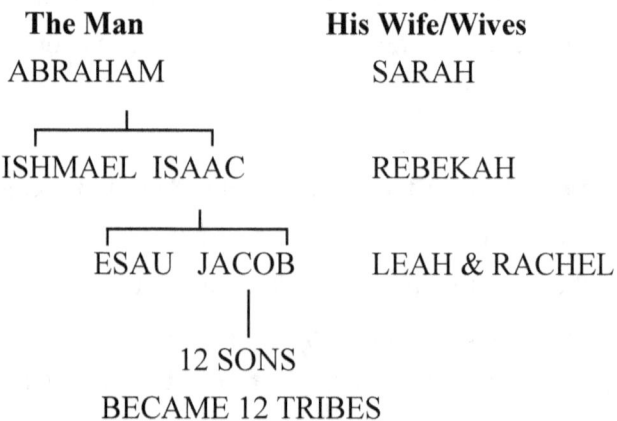

Chapter 2

# THE EXODUS

The period of the Exodus from Egypt and the wanderings in the wilderness is in four books of the Bible: Exodus, Leviticus, Numbers, and Deuteronomy. It extends over the lifetime of Moses. He was born in 1527 BC and died in 1407 BC. During most of this period, the Children of Israel were nomads wandering from place to place like the Patriarchs before them.

## In Egypt

This period begins with the Children of Israel in Egypt (Ex 1:1-15:21).

*The Birth of Moses (Ex. 2:1-10)* Pharaoh commanded that all males born to Hebrew women be cast in the Nile (Ex. 1:22). When Moses' mother put him in a floating crib, he was rescued by Pharaoh's daughter, who, without realizing who the woman was, paid Moses' mother to rear him. Many of the personal names of the Levites and the Aaronites are of Egyptian origin, including the name Moses.

*The Call of Moses (Ex. 3:1-4:31)* God called Abraham to found the nation; He called Moses to deliver and develop the nation.

When Moses was forty years old, God called him to deliver the Children of Israel from the oppression and slavery of Egypt. Like Abraham, who tried to accomplish God's will by utilizing his plan, Moses, in a premature effort at deliverance, killed one of the Egyptians. As a result, he had to flee from the wrath of Pharaoh. He spent the next forty years in the Arabian Desert. This allowed him to learn the desert, knowledge he would need years later as he led the children of Israel through it. He also, no doubt, learned to commune with God during those years. At the foot of Mt. Horeb, God appeared to Moses in a burning bush. Mt. Horeb is another name for Mt. Sinai.

*The Plagues (Ex. 7:14-11:10)* Pharaoh was unwilling to let the children of Israel leave Egypt. After all, why should he give up free slave labor? So, God applied a little persuasion. He used ten plagues to persuade Pharaoh to let the children of Israel leave. The ten plagues were: 1) water turned into blood, 2) frogs, 3) lice, 4) flies, 5) myriad of beasts, 6) boils upon men and beasts, 7) hail, 8) locusts, 9) darkness, 10) death of the firstborn. Each of these was a judgment on one of the Egyptian gods.

*The Passover (Ex. 12:1-13:16).* In the final plague, God judged the land of Egypt with the death of the firstborn in every family. To preserve and protect the Hebrew children, He instructed the Israelites to slay a lamb and sprinkle its blood over the doorposts of their houses. He promised that the death angel would pass over every house where the blood was on the doorposts.

*The Exodus (Ex. 13:17-15:21)* Finally, the haughty Egyptians, humbled and humiliated, allowed the Israelites to leave. Extensive preparation had to be made to remove such a great multitude. The eight or ten months during which Moses was contending with Pharaoh offered the opportunity for this needed preparation. Ladened with stores of jewelry, apparel, and varied wealth, the Hebrews finally marched out of Egypt.

Then, the Pharaoh changed his mind and sent his troops after the Hebrews. They got as far as the Red Sea when they found themselves in a dilemma. The sea was before them, and Pharaoh's army was behind them. God miraculously parted the waters of the Red Sea to allow them to cross. As Pharaoh's army pursued, the walls of water collapsed, and the army drowned.

According to the chronology present in the Bible, the Exodus occurred in 1447 BC. First Kings 6:1 says Solomon began to build the Temple in the fourth year of his reign, 480 years after the Exodus. American archaeologist Edwin R. Thiele, the scholar who has solved many of the chronological problems in the Old Testament, puts the fourth year of Solomon's reign at 967 BC. Therefore, assuming Thiele's date for the fourth year of Solomon's reign, 1 Kings 6:1 indicates that the Exodus occurred in 1447 BC.

A verse in Judges supports that time frame. Jephthah says the Israelites had been in the land for 300 years (Judges 11:26). The wilderness wanderings lasted forty years (Ex. 16:35). According to Caleb, the conquest took seven years (Judges 14:7, 10). Hence, the Israelites occupied the land beginning in 1400 BC. Three hundred years later was 1107 BC, which fits the time frame for when Jephthah made the statement about being in the land for 300 years.

Thus, the Pharaoh of the oppression who died before the Exodus (Ex. 1:11-14) was Thutmose III and the Pharaoh of the Exodus was his successor Amenhotep II. While there is no direct archaeological evidence for the Exodus (the Pharaohs did not record their defeats), there is corroborating evidence. British archaeologist John Garstang dated the fall of Jericho at about 1400 BC (see the discussion concerning Jericho in the chapter on the conquest) and the Amarna Letters (*ca.* 1400-1350 BC) from Canaan asked Egyptian leaders for help against the Habiru invaders. (See the discussion of the Northern Campaign in the chapter on the conquest.).

Critics, however, argue for a later date, usually about 1290 BC, about ten years after Ramses II began to reign. They claim there is no archaeological evidence that Thutmose III built cities in the Delta region (Ex. 1:11). Granted, there is no evidence that says Thutmose III built in the Delta region, but that does not prove he didn't. Since he had fourteen or more military campaigns in Syria, he likely built barracks for his troops in the Delta region. The tomb of his Vizier Rekhmire at Thebes shows Semitic slaves making and transporting bricks.

Critics also say the Jews built the cities of Pithom and Raamses (Ex. 1:11) and Ramses II did not reign until 1290 BC, but Ramses and other Pharaohs of the 19th dynasty used names employed by the Hyksos kings (*ca.* 1760-1580). So, the Hyksos kings could have built a city named Raamses. Ramses II may have merely rebuilt or enlarged these cities. After all, the archaeological data reveals that Ramses II took credit for the achievements of his predecessors. Besides, hundreds of years before either 1290 BC or 1447 BC, there was a "land of Ramses" (Gen. 47:11).

Critics use other arguments to support a later date, such as a later date for the destruction of Jericho, the Amarna letters, and the conclusions of archaeologists that cities such as Bethel, Lachish, Debir, and Hazor were not destroyed until the thirteenth century. (See the comments on these issues in the Northern Campaign section in the chapter on Conquest.)

A later date for the Exodus makes nonsense out of chronology, not only of 1 Kings 6:1 but for the whole period of the Judges. Besides, the Merneptah Stele (1224 BC) depicts the Hebrews as being settled in Canaan, which fits the earlier date for the Exodus, not the later date. (A stele is a commemorative stone, an upright stone slab engraved with an inscription, and is usually used as a victory monument.)

## In the Wilderness

Having been delivered from the bondage of Egypt, the children of Israel were in the wilderness on their way to the Promised Land, the land of Canaan (Ex. 15:22-18:27).

*The Route (Ex 15:22-18:27)* From Goshen in Egypt, the land of Canaan was about one hundred miles away along an ancient caravan route. The inhabitants along that route were fierce, with cities built like walled fortresses. After years of slavery, the Israelites were unprepared to face such foes. God did not direct them to use the direct route to Canaan. Rather, He directed them southward. After about sixty days of marching, they came to Mt. Sinai.

*The Miracles* The journey was marked by miracles, including 1) the parting of the Red Sea, 2) a pillar of cloud leading them by day, 3) a pillar of fire leading them at night, 4) the bitter waters of Marah being sweetened, 4) manna being given daily, 5) water coming from a smitten rock.

## At Sinai

On the way to Canaan, they paused at Mount Sinai (Ex. 19-40; Lev.; Num. 1:1-10:10), where God made a covenant with Israel (Ex. 34:27; Deut 5:2), known as the Mosaic Covenant. It was accepted (Ex. 19:1-25), given (Ex. 20:1-23:33; see "Book of the Covenant" in Ex. 24:7), and ratified (Ex. 24:1-1-18).

*The Law (Ex. 20:1-23:33)* The covenant included the Mosaic Law. The Mosaic Law was not given for people to be justified. In Genesis, God established that justification is by faith (Gen. 15:6). The Mosaic Law was given to *redeemed* people (Ex. 20:1) and used by God to govern His relationship with His people. It was a unit, though it is often divided into the "moral law" (the Ten Commandments, Ex. 20:1-17; the "tablets of the covenant," Deut 9:9), the "civil law" (Ex. 21:1-23:33), and the "ceremonial law" (Ex. 24:12-31:18; Lev.).

In the nineteenth century, critics said that the Mosaic legislation contained too high a moral standard for his day. Therefore, it must have been written centuries later. Then, in 1901, the Code of

## The Exodus

Hammurabi was discovered in Susa. Hammurabi was a king who reigned for 43 years over an empire in Mesopotamia that stretched from the Persian Gulf along the Tigris and Euphrates Rivers to and including Assyrian cities in the North. His time frame has been debated and revised several times. Most now date him about 1728-1686 BC.

Toward the end of his life, Hammurabi inscribed a legal code in a stone 7.4 feet high, tapering down from 5.4 feet across at the top to 6.4 feet at the bottom. This stele contains 282 laws. The parallels between the Law of Moses and the Code of Hammurabi include capital punishment for kidnapping and selling a person (Ex. 21:16 and Section 14 of the Code), the death penalty for both offenders in adultery (Lev. 20:10 and Section 129), the principle of retaliation (Ex. 21:23ff; Deut. 19:21 and Sections 197, 210, 230), etc. The parallels prove that the Mosaic legislation is not of late origin.

At the same time, there are also differences. Hammurabi does not emphasize spiritual principles as Moses does. In general, the Code places an inferior value on human life as compared to Mosaic Law. In some cases, the Laws of Moses do not demand as severe a punishment as the Code of Hammurabi. For example, Hammurabi requires a tenfold restoration for theft; if the thief cannot pay, he will be put to death. Moses requires a five-fold restoration with no death penalty.

*The Tabernacle (Ex 25:1-31:18; 35:1-40:38)* Moses received instructions from the Lord for building the Tabernacle (Ex. 25:1-31:18), which was to be the center of worship for Israel. After an incident of Israel breaking the covenant by making a golden calf similar to the images they had often seen in Egypt (Ex. 32:1-34:35), the Tabernacle was constructed (Ex. 35:1-40:38). It was a beautiful, carefully crafted, portable structure, which for hundreds of years, continued to be the place of worship for the children of Israel. God dwelt in the Tabernacle's Holy of Holies (Ex. 40:34-35).

## In Wilderness Wanderings

When the Israelites left Sinai, they wandered in the wilderness (Num. 10:11-21:35).

*Journey to Kadesh-Barnea (Num. 10:11-12:16)* Led by the pillar of cloud, the Israelites set out toward Canaan. At the time of the first ripe grapes (our September), they arrived on the southern border of Canaan at a place called Kadesh-Barnea.

*The Sending of the Spies (Num. 13:1-14:45)* God instructed Moses to send twelve spies, one from each tribe, through the whole land. The twelve were unanimous in reporting the land's fertility and its inhabitants' fierceness. The majority, ten of the twelve, concluded the land could not be taken because of the size of the inhabitants. When the people heard that, their hearts melted with fear. Only two of the spies, Caleb and Joshua, withstood the majority, insisting that they could take the land and possess it (Num. 13:30), but they could not persuade the doubting and discouraged people.

## The Exodus

*Wandering in the Wilderness (Num. 15:1-21:35)* Because they refuse to enter the land at Kadesh-Barnea, God decreed that that generation would not enter it. The Israelites lived a nomadic life in the desert for the next thirty-seven and a half years. They did not travel constantly, but they did live an unsettled life, moving periodically.

At one point in the journey, God instructed Moses to speak to the rock so that it might bring forth water for them to drink. In his anger, Moses struck it instead of speaking to it. As a result, God decreed that Moses would not be allowed to enter the land.

Several hundred years ago, critics of the Bible claimed that Moses did not write the Pentateuch because neither Moses nor anyone else living at the time the Bible says he lived could write.

Then, in 1799, Napoleon's soldiers found an inscribed stone at Rashid (Rosetta), Egypt. This black granite stone is about four feet high and two and a half feet wide. The text on the stone is a decree of Ptolemy V Epiphanes from about 200 BC. The stone contains one inscription in three languages, one above the other, in Egyptian hieroglyphics (picture writing using a symbol for each word), Egyptian Demotic (closer to alphabetic writing), and Greek. In 1822, a French linguist, Francois Champollion, used the Greek portion to decipher the two Egyptian scripts, finally making it possible to read Egyptian hieroglyphics.

The Rosetta Stone demonstrates that since Moses was educated in Egypt. he could have written in Egyptian hieroglyphics. Archeologists have uncovered writings from this period in many different languages. Moses could have written in Sumerian,

## A Plane View of The Bible

Babylonian, Akkadian, etc. He wrote the Pentateuch in Hebrew.

Critics have also attacked the credibility of the account of this period, claiming that there are no references in the Egyptian record of the Israelites being in Egypt, that the wilderness could not have supported so many nomads, etc. In the first place, the Pharaohs did not record their defeats. Someone has imagined an inscription saying, "Ramses the Great ... before whom all tremble in awe ... announced that the man Moses had kicked his royal [seat] for all the world to see, thus proving that God is Yahweh and the 2000-year-old culture of Egypt is a lie" (source unknown).

Furthermore, the Israelites were *nomads*. They did not build pyramids in the wilderness; they *wandered* through the wilderness. What are archaeologists supposed to find, tent pegs? Nomads don't leave much behind for archeologists to find thousands of years later. As for the fact that the "barren terrain" of the wilderness could not have supported such a large number of Israelites, the Bible indicates that they did not live off the land; they were fed supernaturally (Ex. 16:12-14).

On the other hand, Egyptian inscriptions contain the names of cities on the Exodus route. There is also corroborating evidence (see the next chapter). In his book *Israel in Egypt* (Oxford University Press, 1996), James K. Hoffmeier points out that the picture portrayed in Genesis 39 through Exodus 15 is compatible with what is known from Egyptian history. For example, Egyptians pressed foreigners into hard labor projects as portrayed in Exodus, and many foreign princes were reared and schooled in the Egyptian court. So, a non-Egyptian like Moses could have been raised in the court.

## In the Plain of Moab

*The Plain of Moab (Num. 22:1-36:13; Deut.)* At last, the children of Israel came to the Plain of Moab on the East Side of the Jordan River. By this time, all those twenty years and older at Kadesh-Barnea had died. In the book of Deuteronomy, Moses reminds the second generation that God had given them His commandments and he says, "Therefore hear, O Israel and be careful to observe it, that it may be well with you.... Hear, O Israel: The LORD our God, the LORD is one! You shall love the LORD your God with all your heart, with all your soul, and with all your strength" (Deut. 6:3-5). The point of this passage and, in a sense, the whole book of Deuteronomy is that loving obedience leads to blessing.

*The Farewell of Moses (Deut.)* Moses assembled the children of Israel in the Plain of Moab and delivered a series of farewell addresses. Those three sermons are recorded in the book of Deuteronomy (Deut 1:1-30:20).

*The Death of Moses (Deut. 34:1-12)* Moses ascended to the top of Mt. Nebo. From there, he could view the land he was forbidden to enter. He died and God buried him so that no one knew the place of his burial. Jude reveals that Michael, the Archangel, and the devil disputed over the body of Moses (Jude 9).

Joshua was chosen to succeed Moses.

**Summary:** In the period of the Exodus, God used Moses to take the children of Israel from the land of Egypt to the Plain of Moab. He would have taken them into the land at Kadesh-Barnea, but they refused to go. Thus, the Exodus generation died in the wilderness.

Egypt was the most powerful nation on the earth during this period and several of the following periods. See the appendix for a succinct history of Egypt.

In the first historical period, God promised the land to the Patriarchs. In the second, He gave the Jewish people a covenant consisting of the Mosaic Law, a system of moral, civil, and ceremonial (a system of worship) laws.

The spiritual truth is if people whom God has redeemed will lovingly obey Him, it will be well with them; He will bless them. If they do not obey, God will discipline His children (Deut. 6:3-5).

## The Tabernacle

After departing from Egypt, God instructed Moses to build the Tabernacle (Ex. 25-40). The word "tabernacle" means "tent." The Tabernacle consisted of a tent divided into two compartments with a fence around it, but the whole structure (everything inside the fence) is also called the Tabernacle.

The measurements of the various parts of the Tabernacle are in "cubits." The Hebrew word "cubit" means "forearm." A cubit was reckoned as the length of the arm from the point of the elbow to the end of the middle finger. Though there is some debate among scholars, most agree that the cubit referred to in Exodus was 18 inches long. Based on the 18-inch cubit, the Tabernacle (the courtyard created by the fence) was 150 feet long and 75 feet wide with a linen fence 7½ feet high (Ex. 38:9-13). A football field is 300 feet long and 160 feet wide. The Tabernacle itself, the tent, measured 45 feet by 15 feet and was 15 feet high. The text gives the width and length of the boards used in the Tabernacle (Ex. 36:21). The thickness, however, is not mentioned anywhere in the Bible. Josephus says that each of these boards was four fingers thick, except in the two corners of the west end, each a thick cubit.

The Tabernacle was made of boards of acacia wood (Ex. 36:20). Acacia or shittim wood came from the shittah tree, which grew in the deserts of Sinai and around the Dead Sea. The wood from this tree was hard, very heavy, indestructible by insects, and made of fine and beautiful grain. Other materials used in the construction of the Tabernacle included brass, gold, linen, and even goat's hair. Various cloths were used to make the Tabernacle's curtains and coverings (the roof). The shape of the Tabernacle roof has been a subject of debate, some arguing forcefully that it was flat like those of oriental houses, while others contend that it was peaked and slanted like oriental tents.

*The Brazen Altar (Ex. 27:1-8; 38:1-7)* The brazen altar, which stood just inside the entrance of the Tabernacle courtyard (Ex. 40:6, 29), was made of acacia wood and covered with plates of brass. It was five cubits long (7½ feet), five cubits broad (7½ feet), three cubits high (4½ feet), and had four horns at the four corners. It also had brazen rings and staves covered with brass to transport it. On this altar, sacrifices were offered by the people who could go no further into the courtyard.

*The Brazen Laver (Ex. 30:17-21; 38:8)* The brazen laver stood in the courtyard between the brazen altar and the door of the Tabernacle, that is, the tent (Ex. 40:30-32). No description of its shape or size is given, but many believe it was circular. It was made out of the brass mirrors of the women (Ex. 39:8) and was used for the ceremonial washings of the priests.

*The Holy Place (Ex26:31-35)* After the laver came the Tabernacle, the large tent at the back of the courtyard. The tent was divided into two parts. The first compartment, the Holy Place, contained the lampstand, showbread table, and incense altar. Only the priests were allowed inside the Holy Place.

*The Golden Lampstand (Ex. 25:31-40; 37:17-24)* A candlestick stood on the south side of the Holy Place (Ex. 35:31-40). It consisted of a standard with three branches on each side, thus affording room for seven lamps supplied with olive oil. Nothing is known of its size, its base's formation, or the six branches' exact position. Whether the tops of these branches were level or in the form of an arch or whether the branches extended in the same plane or in different planes is not known.

*The Table of Showbread (Ex. 25:23-30; 37:10-16)* The table of showbread was on the north side of the Holy Place (Ex. 36:35). It was made of acacia wood overlaid with gold, two cubits long, one cubit wide, and a cubit and a half high. It had an ornamental cornice of gold around the top and was furnished with rings of gold and gilt staves (Ex. 25:23-28). On top of the table were placed twelve loaves of bread and two rolls. Frankincense was put on the bread, which was changed every Sabbath Day (Lev. 24:5-9).

*The Altar of Incense (Ex. 35:25-29)* In the west end of the Holy Place, near the veil, stood an altar of incense. It was made of acacia wood covered with gold. It was two cubits high, one in length and one in breadth. It also had four "horns" or projections on the four corners at the top, and like the ark and the table of showbread, it had a cornice of gold, rings, and staves for transportation. The rings were of gold and the staves were of acacia wood covered with gold (Ex. 37:25-28).

*The Holy of Holies (Ex. 26:31-35)* The second compartment, the Holy of Holies, contained the Ark of the Covenant. Only the High Priest was allowed inside the Holy of Holies, and only once a year to sprinkle blood as atonement for the sins of the people.

*The Ark of the Covenant (Ex. 25:10-22; 37:1-9)* The sole piece of furniture within the Holy of Holies was the Ark of the Covenant (Ex. 40:3). It was two cubits and a half long, one cubit and a half in length and the same in height. It, too, was made of acacia wood overlaid with gold within and without. An ornamental cornice, or crown of gold, ran around the top. On each corner of the ark was a gold ring; through the rings, two gilded staves were kept for carrying it when the Tabernacle was moved (Ex. 25:10-15).

The ark contained the two tablets of the law (Ex. 25:16). According to Hebrews 9:4, there was, in addition, a golden pot of manna and Aaron's rod that budded.

The cover of the Ark of the Covenant was of solid gold and called the "mercy seat" (Ex. 25:17, 21). Two golden cherubim with outstretched wings emerged from the ends of this cover (Ex. 25:18-20). No particular description of their size, shape, or general appearance is given here or elsewhere.

The Tabernacle was a type, that is, a God-intended illustration of spiritual truth. The presence of God dwelt in the Holy of Holies. Everything else was instructive in approaching Him. While there are many pictures and symbols throughout the Tabernacle (some "interpretations" of these go too far), the major message of the Tabernacle is in the furniture.

| | |
|---|---|
| The Brazen Altar | Conversion |
| The Brazen Laver | Cleansing |
| The Holy Place | Communion |
| The Lampstand | Christ is the light of the world. He is our light. |
| The Showbread | Christ is the bread of life. He is our food. |
| The Altar of Incense | Christ is the intercessor. He is our Advocate. |

## The Offerings

The Lord instructed that various offerings could be presented to Him at the Tabernacle. The Brazen Altar was the place of sacrifice. There were five "offerings" given at this altar.

*The Burnt Offering (Lev. 1:1-17; 6:8-13)* The animals for the burnt offering were bullocks, sheep, goats, turtledoves, and young pigeons. If Israelites making this voluntary offering were offering a bullock, they would put their hand on the victim's head and slay the animal. The priest took the blood and sprinkled it around the altar. After the blood was sprinkled, the Israelites flayed the animal and cut it into pieces. In later history, priests and Levites sometimes did this (2 Chron. 29:34). Priests burned the entire offering. The ceremony was slightly changed if the offering consisted of a goat, sheep, or fowl. The burnt offering was the only one that was entirely burnt. Thus it is sometimes called "the whole" burnt offering (Deut. 33:10; etc.). The burning was to be so gradual that it would last from morning to evening or from one daily sacrifice to the next. The Lord commanded that the fire on the altar should never go out.

The purpose of the burnt offering is never clearly stated in the Scripture. Some Jewish scholars contend that it was for evil thoughts, while others believe that it was for the violation of affirmative precepts. Most Christian interpreters see this as a voluntary act of worship, an act of dedication of one's whole life to the Lord.

*The Meal Offering (Lev. 2:1-16; 6:14-23)* The meal offering was wholly vegetable. It could be fine flour, flour baked into cakes, or even dried ears of corn. Sometimes, it was present in its raw form and other times, it was baked. In either case, specific directions were given concerning the ceremony observed. No blood was involved in this offering. The fire only consumed a portion of the meal offering. The rest was given to the priests. Neither leaven nor honey was to be mixed with it. The meal offering usually accompanied and was subsidiary to the sin and burnt offerings, and the quality offered differed according to the victim presented as a burnt offering (Num. 15:4-9).

To the Jews in Moses' day, this was probably an act of worship, which indicated a consecration of the fruit of their hands and acknowledgment of God's provision. Believers often see the meal offering as a symbol of the life and perfection of Jesus Christ.

*The Peace Offering (Lev. 3:1-17; 7:11-38)* There were three kinds of peace offerings: 1) a thanks offering, 2) a free-will offering, and 3) an offering for vows (Lev. 7:12, 16). It was either of the herd or flock and either male or female (Lev. 3:1, 7, 12). The blood was sprinkled around the altar and the fat and parts were burnt. When offered for a thanksgiving offering, a meal offering was presented with it (Lev. 7:12-13).

A peculiarity of the peace offering was that the breast of the animal was waved and the shoulder was heaved (Lev. 7:34). According to Jewish tradition, parts of the sacrifice were laid on the hands of the one offering the sacrifice. The priest put his hand underneath the hands of the one making the offering and moved them in a horizontal direction for the waving and a vertical direction for the heaving. This was a presentation of the parts to God. The breast and the shoulder went to the priest (Lev. 7:31-34). The remainder of the victim, except that which was burnt, was consumed by the one making the sacrifice and his family under certain restrictions (Lev. 7:19-21). It was the only one of the five offerings in which the one making the sacrifice partook of it.

To the Jews who participated in this offering, it was an act of communion and thanksgiving. Believers see it as a type of Christ as our priest.

*The Sin Offering (Lev. 4:1-5:1; 6:24-30)* There were two kinds of sin offerings, one for the whole congregation and the other for individuals. For the former, a young bullock was burnt in the outer court of the Tabernacle, where the elders laid hands on its head, and it was killed. The high priest then took the blood into the Holy Place and sprinkled it seven times before the veil, putting some on the horns of the golden altar of incense. The remainder of the blood was poured out at the foot of the altar of burnt offering. The fat of the animal was burnt upon the altar, and the rest of the body was taken outside the camp and burned (Lev. 4:13-21).

There were three types of sin offerings for the individual. The first was for the high priest; the ceremony varied only slightly from that described. (Lev. 4:3-12). The second sin offering was for the rulers. In this case, a kid was killed instead of a bullock. The priest did not enter into the Holy Place but merely put some of the blood on the horns of the altar of burnt offering and poured the rest out by the foot of the altar. The fat was burned upon the altar (Lev. 4:22-26). The third was for the people. A female kid or lamb was brought and treated as in the case just described (Lev. 4:27-35). If poverty prevented procuring a kid or lamb, two turtledoves or two young pigeons could be substituted. For the very poorest, a small offering of fine flour could be substituted (Lev. 5:7-13).

The sin offering was offered for the sins of ignorance against negative precepts (Lev. 4:2, 13:22-27). This offering demonstrated to the Jews in ancient times the need to shed blood for the atonement of sins. Christians see in it a picture of the shedding of the blood of Christ as a payment for all sin.

*The Trespass Offering (Lev. 5:14-6:7; 7:1-10)* The trespass offering was similar to the sin offering, yet there were several significant differences. In the trespass offering, lambs were offered, and the blood was sprinkled around the altar of burnt offering (Lev. 5:18; 7:2). The priest was required to make a special valuation of the ram offered (Lev. 5:15, 16).

The trespass offering was offered in cases of trespass committed in holy things: dishonesty or falsehood in a trust, robbery adjoined with deceit, dishonesty, and falsehood about things found (Lev. 5:15-6:7). This offering demonstrates the need for restitution.

**Summary**: The Mosaic Law called for five different offerings, the first three of which are called "sweet" and the last two "non-sweet." All were undoubtedly done as a memorial (Lev. 6:15). These offerings were a memorial to the Jews as the Lord's Table and baptism are a memorial for Christians today. Perhaps the first three offerings speak most clearly of conversion and the last two of the Christian life.

## The Festivals

In addition to the offerings, various feasts or festivals were observed during the year. Leviticus 23 lists the seven annual feasts of Israel.

*The Passover (Lev. 23:4-5)* Passover was to be observed on the fourteenth day of the first month, the month Abib, or, as it was subsequently called, Nisan, corresponding to March/April. It commemorated the passing over of the houses of the Israelites by the death angel at the time when the firstborn of Egypt was slain.

During Passover, great care was taken to abstain from leaven. A he-lamb or kid of the first year was selected by the head of the family and was slain. Its blood was sprinkled originally on the doorposts but subsequently on the bottom of the altar. The animal was roasted with fire and eaten with unleavened bread and a salad of bitter herbs. It could not be boiled, nor was a bone to be broken. When they first ate the Passover in Egypt, the Israelites had their own loins girded and their shoes on, ready for a journey, and they partook of it, standing as if in haste to leave. In the following years, the position was changed to sitting or reclining. This feast was fulfilled at the cross, Christ being the Passover sacrifice (1 Cor. 5:7).

*The Feast of Unleavened Bread (Lev. 23:6-8)* The Feast of Unleavened Bread followed immediately after the Passover and lasted seven days, the first month from the 15$^{th}$ to the 22$^{nd}$ day. Each day after the morning sacrifice, a sacrifice in connection with the feast was presented. Unleavened bread alone was eaten (Ex. 12:15-20; 13:6-8; Deut. 16:3-8). The first and seventh days of the feast were celebrated by a holy convocation and a rest from work, except for food preparation. On the intervening days, work might be carried on unless the weekly Sabbath fell on one of them, in which case the full strictness of Sabbath-keeping was observed. On the second feast day, the first half of the new harvest was symbolically waved, not burnt on the altar, as an offering to the Lord, accompanied by a lamb of the first year for burnt offering with its meat and drink offerings. This feast was perhaps fulfilled with the burial of Christ (1 Cor. 5:6-8).

*The Feast of First Fruits (Lev. 23:9-14)* The feast of First Fruits was observed in the first month on the sixteenth day. Offerings were given to express gratitude to God for the harvest. Christ was the first fruit of the resurrection, a sample of what would come (1 Cor. 15:23).

*The Feast of Pentecost (Lev. 23:15-22)* The first three feasts were to be observed in the first month. Pentecost was to be observed in the third month, fifty days after Passover. The Scriptures do not attach any historical significance to this festival but seem to teach that Pentecost owes its origin to the harvest, which terminated at this time. The Holy Spirit came on the day of the Feast of Pentecost (Acts 2:1).

*The Feast of Trumpets (Lev. 23:23-25)* The Feast of Trumpets was the first of three feasts to be observed in the seventh month. It began on the first day of the seventh month, Tisri (October/November). It was Israel's New Year. The day was kept as a

## The Exodus

Sabbath, with no work being performed. The usual daily morning sacrifice was offered, then the monthly sacrifice of the new moon, and then the sacrifice particular to the day, which consisted of a bullock, a ram, seven lambs for a burnt offering, and a kid for a sin-offering (Num. 29:1-6). This perhaps pictures the re-gathering of Israel at the Second Coming of Christ.

*The Day of Atonement (Lev. 23:26-32)* The great Day of Atonement was observed on the tenth day of the seventh month, Tisri, corresponding to our September/October. It was a day of great solemnity, designed and kept as a feast day. On this day, the high priest, clad in plain white linen garments, brought for himself a young bullock for a sin offering and a ram for a burnt offering and for the people, two young goats for a sin offering and a ram for a burnt offering. The two goats were brought before the door of the Tabernacle and, by the casting of lots, one was designated as a sacrifice and the other as a scapegoat. The high priest slaughtered the bullock and made a sin offering for himself and his family. He next entered the Holy Place for the first time, bearing a censer with burning coals, and he filled the place with incense. Then, entering the Holy Place a second time, he sprinkled blood before the mercy seat. Next, he killed the goat, which was for the people's sin offering and entering the Holy Place a third time, sprinkled its blood, as he had sprinkled that of the bullock.

Some of the blood of the two animals was then put on the horns of the altar of the incense and sprinkled on the altar itself.

After this, the high priest, putting his hands on the head of the scapegoat, confessed the sins of the people and sent the goat off into the wilderness. Then, he washed himself, changed his garments, arrayed himself in a beautiful robe of his high office, and offered the two rams as a burnt offering for himself and the people. The Day of Atonement celebrated Israel's national salvation. It was also a prophecy for the future salvation of Israel.

*The Feast of Tabernacles (Lev. 23:33-44)* The Feast of Tabernacles was observed in the seventh month from the 15$^{th}$ to the 22$^{nd}$ day. It was instituted to remind the people that their fathers dwelt in tents in the wilderness (Lev. 23:43) and also to be an annual thanksgiving for all of the products of the earth: corn, fruit, wine, and oil were gathered for the year (Lev. 23:39). During the eight days of this feast, the people dwelt in booths made of branches of palms and other trees. On each day, they sacrificed two rams, fourteen lambs and a kid for a burnt offering. During the continuance of the feast, seventy bullocks were offered, thirteen on the first day, twelve on the second, eleven on the third, and so on, the number being diminished by one each day until the seventh day when only seven were offered. The eighth day was a day of particular solemnity and had for its special offering a bullock, a ram and seven lambs for a burnt offering and a goat for a sin offering (Deut. 29:12-38). On the Sabbatical Year, the Feast of Tabernacles was still further celebrated by a public reading of the law (Deut. 31:10-13). Perhaps this feast pictures the Kingdom.

**Summary:** The Mosaic Law required the Jews to observe seven annual festivals. Four were bunched together at the beginning of the year (three in the first month and one in the third month). The other three occurred later in the year during the seventh month.

Israel's annual feasts were similar to our holidays. To be more specific and accurate, they were more like our Easter and Christmas. These holidays were holy days; they signified and symbolized spiritual truths to the Jews. These festivals were also prophecies. The first four were fulfilled at Christ's first coming, and the last three will be fulfilled when Christ comes again.

The book of Leviticus is filled with civil and ceremonial rules and regulations, which became "customs" throughout Israel's history. For example, Leviticus 15:4 speaks of the Sabbatical Year, and Leviticus 15:10 speaks of the Year of Jubilee, etc.

Chapter 3

# THE CONQUEST

The Conquest began in 1407 BC. According to Joshua 14:7, 10, it was completed in seven years. Thus, this period ended in 1400 BC, although it probably extended a few years beyond that. For a few years, Elders ruled in Israel. After that, God raised up Judges.

## Preparation for Conquest

*The Crossing of the Jordan (Josh. 1:1-4:24)* After the death of Moses, the Lord instructed Joshua to lead the children of Israel into the Promised Land. In preparation, God told him, "This Book of the Law shall not depart from your mouth, but you shall meditate in it day and night, that you may observe to do according to all that is written in it. For then you will make your way prosperous, and then you will have good success (Josh. 1:8).

To enter the land, they had to cross the Jordan River. It was the worst time of the year for such a crossing because it was during the flood season when the Jordan overflowed its banks. As God parted the waters of the Red Sea for Moses, so He parted the waters of the Jordan for Joshua and Israel to march across.

*The Observance of the Law (Josh. 5:1-15)* Once in the land, the people were circumcised and the Passover was observed. At this point, the manna, which God had miraculously and mercifully given during the wilderness journey, ceased.

## The Central Campaign

The children of Israel did not begin the conquest from the south end or the north end of the land. Rather, they entered the land from the east about in the middle. (The Mediterranean Sea borders the west side.) Once in the land, they turned south. Then they went north. In other words, their initial conquest divided the land into two parts and they conquered one part at a time. This is known as a "divide and conquer" military strategy. It is still studied and used.

*Jericho (Josh. 6:1-27)* After the children of Israel had crossed the Jordan River, they camped at Gilgal. This became Joshua's headquarters. Now, they had to begin to take the land. The first city in their path was Jericho. This strongly fortified city in the plain of the Jordan commanded the passes that led up to the land of Canaan. Hence, it was the first object of attack.

By this time, the news of the divine intervention in the parting of the Red Sea, the conquering of the kings in the Trans-Jordan, and the parting of the waters of the Jordan had sent a great fear into the hearts of the inhabitants of Jericho. The city's rulers ordered the gates to be shut and the city to be secured.

## The Conquest

God directed Joshua to circle the city, led by the priests and the ark, each day for six days and seven times on the seventh day. Then, the people sounded their trumpets and gave a mighty shout, and God supernaturally knocked over the walls of Jericho. Israel marched in and possessed the city.

Because Rahab had concealed the spies, she and her family were spared. According to James, she was justified by her works. James is not teaching that a person gets to heaven by works. He teaches justification by faith (Jas. 2:23). He also teaches works are profitable (Jas. 2:14-17); they perfect faith (Jas. 2:18-23, especially 2:22), and they enable others to perceive one's faith (Jas. 2:24-26; "you see" in Jas. 2:24; that is, man sees faith by works). Thus, there is a justification by works, as well as a justification by faith.

If this sounds confusing, perhaps Romans 4:2 will clear up the fog. It says, "For if Abraham were justified by works, he had something of which to boast, but not before God." In other words, there is a justification by faith *before God*, and there is a justification by works *before men*. In Genesis 15:6, Abraham believed God, which was accounted to him for righteousness. That was justification by faith (Jas. 2:23; Rom. 4:1-3). In Genesis 22, he offered Isaac upon the altar. That was justification by works (Jas. 2:21).

When John Garstang excavated Jericho from 1930 to 1936, he identified different archaeological levels that had been built on the site over several centuries. He named these alphabetically, beginning with a level he dated about 3000 BC. Garstang said city "D," constructed around 1500 BC, was destroyed by an earthquake *ca.* 1400 BC. (Earthquakes are called "acts of God.") He concluded an earthquake destroyed it because the walls fell outward. He said it was around 1400 BC because out of the 150,000 pieces of pottery found there, only one was of the Mycenean type, which began to be imported into Palestine in abundance from 1400 BC onward. Moreover, numerous scarabs (the representation of a beetle regarded as sacred by the ancient Egyptians) were found in the burial grounds, but none were later than the two of Amenhotep III, and there was no evidence from his successor, Amenhotep IV's reign, which is distinctive and plentiful.

Since then, Garstang's dating of the destruction of Jericho has been debated. In 1952, Kathleen M. Kenyon began her work at Jericho. She concluded that the walls of city "D" should be dated about 2300 BC and that it is impossible to be certain when Jericho fell. A carbon-14 test, however, put the date at 1410 BC. (Bryant Wood, "Did the Israelites Conquer Jericho?" *Archaeological Review*, March/April 1990.)

*Ai (Josh. 7:1-8:29)* The next city to be taken in the central campaign was Ai. Many believe that Ai was simply a military outpost of Bethel. Without getting specific directions from God, Joshua chose 3,000 men and marched up a mountain slope to attack. To their surprise, they were pushed back by the men of Ai, who chased them down the slope and slew thirty-six of them.

Joshua and the Elders cried to God and He revealed to them that the defeat was due to sin. In the destruction of Jericho, Achan had disobeyed the divine command and took some of the spoils of war for himself. Under the direction of God, Achan, the offender, was found and punished. Having put away the sin and now following the Lord's direction, the children of Israel could conquer Ai.

It is worth noting that the children of Israel conquered Jericho with the aid of God's supernatural power, but in the conquest of Ai, they used military strategy and strength. Part of their army approached the city, while most of the army hid behind it. When the first part fled, the army of Ai in the city pursued them. The Israelite forces behind the city were able to take it. God rarely uses the same method twice. He is creative. He uses different means to accomplish His purpose. Sometimes, the means are supernatural; often, they are not.

*The Ratification of the Law (Josh. 8:30-35)* Moses had instructed Joshua to ratify the law once they reached Shechem. After conquering Ai, the children of Israel did just that. Half of the tribes stood on Mt. Ebal and the other half on Mt. Gerizim. Those on Mt. Gerizim declared the blessings and those on Mt. Ebal proclaimed the cursings. Thus, in a solemn fashion, Israel was to serve God in the land and hear and ratify the covenant.

## The Southern Campaign

*The Gibeonites (Josh. 9:1-27)* By pretending to be inhabitants of a far-distant land, the Gibeonites were able to deceive Joshua and the leaders and secure an alliance with Israel. In deference to the oath that they had taken, Joshua spared the Gibeonites, though there was a penalty for their deception. They were made of hewers of wood and drawers of water.

*A Plane View of The Bible*

*The Southern City-States (Josh. 10:1-43)* When the southern city-states learned that the people of Gibeon had made an alliance with the Israelites, they marched against the city of Gibeon. In response to an urgent appeal from the Gibeonites, Joshua, with his whole force, hurriedly marched and defeated the southern kings.

During the southern campaign, God supernaturally intervened by raining hail on the enemy and causing the sun to "standstill" for more daylight so that Joshua could completely destroy them. Joshua 10:13 says, "The sun stood still and the moon stooped." Did the sun actually stand still and the moon stop? Stopping the sun from moving would not give more daylight because the earth rotates the sun. To provide more daylight, the rotation of the earth would have to stop.

This is the language of observation. It is how things appear on the earth. Even scientists speak of the sunset when they know that the sun does not actually "set;" the earth is just rotating around the sun. Perhaps the rotation of the earth on its axis, which would not affect the movement of the earth around the sun, was slowed. Whatever actually occurred physically, God supernaturally did something unique (Josh. 10:14) to give Joshua more daylight and, thus, more time to finish the battle.

Archaeologists have excavated cities conquered in the southern campaign, including Lachish (Josh. 10:31-34) and Debir (Josh. 10:38-39; etc.). Excavations of Lachish indicate that it was *completely* destroyed by fire around 1230 BC (Albright's date; Ussishkin puts it at 1150 BC) and that Debir was not destroyed until 1200 BC. Critics claim these dates prove that the Exodus and

*The Conquest*

the subsequent conquest must have been in the thirteenth century BC, not the fifteenth.

The account in Joshua, however, does not say that the Israelites *completely* destroyed all the cities they conquered. For example, Joshua 10:32 only speaks of the slaughter of the inhabitants of Lachish, not the destruction of the city (the same is true of Debir; Josh. 10:38-39). These cities, which Joshua defeated, may have been re-inhabited and later destroyed. Actually, the dates for the destruction of these cities are debated, but there is no doubt that these cities existed at the time of the conquest.

## The Northern Campaign

When the kings of the north learned of Joshua's victory in the south, they gathered their forces together and determined to defeat Joshua. But Joshua, strengthened by the Lord, hastened northward and was able to defeat not only Hazor but all the kings of the north (Josh. 11:1-15). The book of Joshua specifically says that Hazor "was burned with fire" (Josh. 11:11). Archaeologists disagree on the date, but there is overwhelming evidence that Hazor was, in fact, destroyed by fire.

There is evidence that the children of Israel invaded Palestine during the fifteenth century BC. In 1886, peasant women discovered hundreds of clay tablets in Amarna, Egypt, a town about 200 miles south of Cairo. The tablets known as the Amarna Letters contain diplomatic correspondence between vassal governors in Canaan and their Egyptian Lords from about 1400 BC to 1370 BC.

These letters report an invasion from the Habiru, a word which means "one who passes through" (the land). Since the discovery of the Amarna Letters, the name "Habiru" has been found in other places. From all these references, it is apparent that the term Habiru is used in a variety of ways, including the use of nomads, soldiers, servants, and foreigners. It came to be used generally for enemies or simply in a pejorative sense of people the writer did not like ("a bad name to call one's enemies").

While there is no consensus among scholars, some have concluded that the Habiru of the Amarna Letters are Hebrews. Habiru may be the linguistic equivalent of Hebrew. The word "Hebrew" is not widely used in the Old Testament, but in several places, it is used by foreigners to refer to the Israelites (Ex. 2:6; 1 Sam. 13:19).

Beyond the linguistic issue, there is evidence in the Amarna Letters that Habiru were the Hebrews of the conquest. There is no communication from the first conquered cities: Jericho, Bethel, Beersheba, Gibeon, and Hebron. The correspondence from Megiddo indicates that the towns in the region of Arad in the south had already fallen, which agrees with Numbers 21:1-3. Gezer, Ashkelon, and Lachish are other cities listed as already fallen, which were captured early in the conquest.

In general, these letters picture disunity among the kings of Canaan and some forsaking their allegiance to Egypt for an alliance with the invader. One letter reads, "The Habiru plunder all the lands of the king. If there are archers in this year, the lands of the king, my lord, will remain, but if there are no archers in the land of the king, my lord will be lost." In other words, a Canaanite king at the time of Joshua pleads with the king of Egypt to send troops (archers), or all will be lost because of the Habiru invaders. That was precisely the situation when Joshua was subduing the central portion of Canaan. The Egyptian Pharaoh could not send help because his army had been destroyed in the Exodus. In the letter from the Jerusalem king, he accuses Shechem of defecting to the Habiru cause, saying, "or shall we do like Labayu, who gave the land of Shechem to the Habiru." According to the book of Joshua, the Israelites assembled between Mount Ebal and Mount Gerizim near Shechem (Josh. 8:30-35).

Critics have interpreted the Amarna letters to argue for a late date of the Exodus. For example, the letters from King Abdi-Heba of Jerusalem indicate that his city is in danger of capture, but the critics argue that 2 Samuel 5:6-7 shows that the Israelites did not capture Jerusalem until David's time. Therefore, the critics say the Habiru could not have been the Israelites.

The problem with that interpretation is that neither the Amarna letters nor the book of Joshua state that Jerusalem was captured or destroyed. According to Scripture, Joshua defeated the Jerusalemite troops along with their allies from Hebron, Jarmuth, Lachish, and Eglon at the battle of Gibeon. Adoni-Zedek, the king of Jerusalem, was killed (Josh. 10:1-27). Jerusalem itself was not captured until after Joshua's death (Judges 1:8) and even then, not all the Jebusites were killed (Judges 1:21). Much later, David conquered Jerusalem.

Nothing in the Amarna account cannot be reconciled with the Joshua record. The Amarna Letter, from the Canaanites themselves, records the Israelite conquest of Canaan about 1400 BC. This archaeological discovery confirms the account of the conquest under Joshua.

## The Division of the Land

After Joshua conquered the land, it was divided among the twelve tribes.

*East of the Jordan (Josh. 13:8-33)* Moses had promised Reuben, Gad, and half the tribe of Manasseh the Trans-Jordan. Joshua allotted them the land promised to them.

*West of the Jordan (Josh. 14:1-19:51).* The rest of the land was divided as follows: in the South were Simeon, Judah, Benjamin, and Dan. In the center were Ephraim and Manasseh and in the North were Issachar, Zebulun, Asher, and Naphtali.

*The Cities of Refuge (Josh. 20:1-21:42)* For those who accidentally or unintentionally killed someone, cities of refuge were established.

## The Charge of Joshua

*Dismissal of the Eastern Tribes (Josh. 22:1-34)* With a challenge and a celebration, the tribes that settled east of the Jordan were sent to their portion of the land.

## The Conquest

*Farewell of Joshua (Josh. 23:1-24:33)* Joshua was an old man by this time. He gathered everyone together at Shechem and charged them to follow the Lord.

**Summary:** Under the hand of Joshua, the children of Israel entered the central part of the land and conquered it. Then, they conquered the south and the north.

One of the great spiritual truths from this period is that the children of God should constantly meditate on the Word of God so that they might obey it and thus be successful in doing God's will (Josh. 1:8). Obedience leads to victory.

It is also interesting to note that during this period:

They had to fight, yet God supernaturally gave them victory.
They had to deal with sin before God gave them victory.
They had to fight continually before God gave them victory.
In a similar fashion, we struggle, and yet God gives us victory.

Chapter 4

# THE JUDGES

During this period, judges, who were not "judges" in the modern American sense of the term, ruled Israel. The Hebrew word translated "judge" means "to judge, govern." A judge in ancient Israel was God's agent (Judges 2:16) who governed the people in civil, religious, and political affairs as well as sometimes, though not always, acting as a military commander.

This rather extended period, about a third of the time from Moses to Malachi, begins about 1375 BC and stretches to 1043 BC. Except for Gideon and Samuel, the judges did not rule over all twelve tribes or govern one right after the other, like the Presidents of the United States. They served over different locations, and most had overlapping years of service, more like the governors of the United States. Thus, it is impossible to divide this time into successive periods, like the period of the Exodus, or even into successive men, like the period of the Patriarchs.

## The Characteristics of the Period

Preceded by the magnificent period of the Conquest and followed by the glorious days of the Kingdom, the period of the Judges has been likened to a valley between two mountain peaks. The Conquest was the period of success; Judges is the period of failure. Several verses at the beginning of the book of Judges capture the essence of this period. "They forsook the LORD and served Baal and the Ashtoreths. And the anger of the LORD was hot against Israel. So He delivered them into the hands of plunderers who despoiled them; and He sold them into the hands of their enemies all around, so that they could no longer stand before their enemies. Wherever they went out, the hand of the LORD was against them for calamity, as the LORD had said, and as the LORD had sworn to them. And they were greatly distressed. Nevertheless, the LORD raised up judges who delivered them out of the hand of those who plundered them" (Judges 2:13-16)

There is a repeated cycle during this period. Judges 2:11-19 spells it out in four steps.

*Sin (Judges 2:11-13)* The children of Israel did evil in the sight of the Lord. They forsook Him, disobeyed Him, and worse yet, they became idolaters.

*Slavery (Judges 2:14-15)* The Lord became angry with Israel. As a result, He delivered them into the hands of their enemy. They became the slaves of the inhabitants of the land.

*Supplication (Judges 2:15)* Once the children of Israel were conquered and captured by their enemies, they began to cry out to the Lord for deliverance.

*Salvation (Judges 2:16)* When the children of Israel sought the Lord, He raised up "judges" to deliver them from their enemies. Judges were civilians and, sometimes, military rulers who delivered and ruled over the people. Actually, the Lord ruled directly through them, not indirectly through a king, as he did in the period of the Kingdom. There was no central government (hence, no hierarchy) and no standing army. Since the days of Josephus, this period has been called "the theocracy," that is, God ruled directly.

These were the dark ages of Israel's history. Spirituality was at a low ebb. The sacrifices and the sacred festivals were sadly neglected. Israel was frequently defeated.

## The Characters of the Period

*Othniel (Judges 3:5-11)* Othniel was the younger brother of Caleb. He defeated the kings of Mesopotamia and ruled over Israel for forty years.

*Ehud (Judges 3:12-30)* This left-handed Benjaminite slew Eglon, king of the Moabites, and delivered Israel from Moab. Then, the land rested for eighty years.

*Shamgar (Judges 3:31)* He delivered Israel from the Philistines, on one occasion slaying 600 with an ox goad.

*Deborah (Judges 4:1-5:31)* After the Canaanites had opposed Israel for twenty years, reducing the people to abject slavery, Deborah called them to arms. She inspired them to rise under the leadership of Barak and throw off the yoke of oppression. She easily ranks among the greatest of the judges and one of the noblest women in history.

*Gideon (Judges 6:1-8:32).* When Israel again lapsed into idolatry, the Lord raised up the Midianites to afflict them. Over seven years, these oppressors came in great numbers and impoverished the land, destroying crops and livestock. In this dire extremity, God raised up Gideon. Gideon's army was reduced from 32,000 men to 10,000 and then to 300. This handful of men defeated the Midianites. Gideon and Samuel were the only judges who ruled over all twelve tribes.

*Abimelech (Judges 8:33-9-57)* Gideon's son ruled from Shechem for three years. Actually, he was made king by the men of Shechem (9:6) rather than being raised up as a judge by God.

*Tola (Judges 10:1-2)* This man governed Israel for twenty-three years.

*Jair (Judges 10:3-5)* With his son, he ruled for twenty-three years.

*Jephthah (Judges 10:6-12:7)* When the Ammonites oppressed the land, Israel asked Jephthah to become their leader.

Before going to battle, he vowed that if God gave him victory, on his return, he would offer as a sacrifice whatever first came out of his house (Judges 11:31). He probably had an animal in mind ("it'), but when he gained a decisive victory and returned home, he was shocked to see his daughter and only child coming to greet him. The brave girl readily yielded, and the father seemed to fulfill his vow. Given that the law forbade human sacrifice (Lev. 18:21; Deut. 12:29-31), it is highly unlikely that he did that. Rather, she remained single for the rest of her life (Judges 11:36-39, especially the comment that "she knew no man").

*Ibzan (Judges 12:8-10)* Ibzan was judge over Israel for seven years.

## The Judges

*Elon (Judges 12:11-12)* Elon judged Israel for ten years.

*Abdon (Judges 12:13-15)* Abdon continued as a judge for eight years.

*Samson (Judges 13:1-16:31)* Endowed with super-human strength, Samson fought against the Philistines. First, he defeated them; later, they defeated him. Rather than a leader or a general, he was a hero. For twenty years, he accomplished what God desired, but he was not without his faults.

*Eli (1 Sam. 1:1-4:22)* This leader was both High Priest and judge. He was a man of marked personal piety. His chief fault, however, was that he indulged the vices of his sons to such an extent that they ended up in failure and crime.

*Samuel (1 Sam.)* Hannah was a devout but barren woman. So, she prayed until God gave her a child. That child was the saintly Samuel. He ranks with Abraham, Moses, and David as one of the noblest characters in Bible history. He was the last and greatest of the judges. He founded the School of the Prophets, which wielded a wide influence in Israel for hundreds of years. As a judge, reformer, statesman, writer, and especially a man mighty in prayer, he left his impression deep in the nation's heart.

The most significant archaeological discovery concerning this period was found in Egypt. In 1895, Flinders Petrie discovered the Merneptah Stele at Thebes, Egypt. It consists of a poem describing the victories of Merneptah (*ca.* 1224-1216 BC) over Libya and other lands, including Palestine. It contains the lines:

> Canaan is plundered with every evil;
> Askalon is conquered; Gezer is held;

Yenoan is made a thing of naught;
Israel is destroyed; it has no seed corn;
Palestine has become a widow of Egypt.
All lands are united in peace ....

This is the oldest occurrence of the word "Israel" found anywhere. It is written with a symbol that denotes "people" rather than "land," which implies the sedentary occupation of western Palestine. This indicates that Israel was settled in the land *ca.* 1220 BC. The Scripture makes no mention of this raid by Merneptah.

**Summary:** During these dark days, Israel continually lapsed into sin and God raised up Judges to deliver them.

Ruth's beautiful and romantic story falls in the time frame of the period of the Judges. Driven out of Israel by famine, Naomi and her family went to the land of Moab. While there, one of her sons married Ruth. After the death of her husband and sons, Naomi decided to return to the land of her father. Ruth followed her mother-in-law with a rare devotion and returned to Bethlehem with her. Later, she married Boaz and became the great-grandmother of David and an ancestor of Jesus Christ.

The spiritual lesson from this time is that sin produces slavery. Jesus said, "Whosoever sins becomes the slave of sin" (Jn. 8:34). When you are a slave to sin, you are *not* free to *not sin*. People do what they want to do, thinking that they will be free, but the opposite is true. Disobedience leads to defeat. Repeated sin leads to servitude. Yet when sinful people turn (return) to the Lord, He graciously hears and delivers. Jesus said, "You shall know the truth and the truth shall make you free" (Jn. 8:33).

Chapter 5

# THE UNITED KINGDOM

The book of Judges concludes with the statement, "In those days there was no king in Israel; everyone did what was right in his own eyes" (Judges 21:25; see also 17:6). When people do that which is right in their eyes, instead of God's, there is not only sin and servitude; there is political chaos. Political confusion led to Israel's desire for a king. This period is called the United Kingdom because, for the first time, a king ruled over Israel.

Several factors led to the anointing of a king and the establishment of the kingdom. For one thing, Samuel's sons failed. Samuel personally ruled Israel long and well, but in contrast to his integrity and dignity, his sons were proving themselves unworthy to succeed their father. Also, the Israelites wanted a king like the other nations around them. So, assembling the nation in Ramah, the home of Samuel, the Elders demanded a king. They reminded Samuel that his sons had not followed in his footsteps.

Samuel took the request to the Lord, Who instructed him to yield to their demand. The Lord told him: "Heed the voice of the people in all that they say to you; for they have not rejected you, but they have rejected Me, that I should not reign over them" (1 Sam. 8:7). Yet God had foreseen this day approaching, for He had given instructions in the Law of Moses concerning when a king would rule over Israel.

If the period of the Judges is the Dark Ages of Israel's history, the period of the United Kingdom is its Golden Age. During the period of the United Kingdom, Israel expanded to its largest extent and reached new heights in agriculture and literature. The United Kingdom's period begins with Saul's inauguration in 1043 BC. It concludes with the division of the Kingdom in 931 BC.

## The Reign of Saul

Saul, who reigned from 1043 BC to 1011 BC, was chosen to be the first king of Israel primarily because he was the kind of man Israel desired. He has been called "a clever man, a great military leader, and an able statesman." Yet he failed because he did not wholly follow the Lord. In 1 Samuel, the accounts of Saul and David are interwoven. The highlights of Saul's life are as follows.

*The Choice of Saul (1 Sam. 9:1-10:27)* Saul was searching for his father's donkeys, who had strayed away from home when he encountered Samuel. Having been directed by God, Samuel anointed Saul king over Israel. When Israel assembled at Mizpah to choose a king, the lot fell upon Saul. He was "taller than any of the people from the shoulders upward" (1 Sam. 10:23).

*The Crowning of Saul (1 Sam. 11:1-15)* After Saul led the nation to victory over the Ammonites, Israel made him king at Gilgal.

*The Disobedience of Saul (1 Sam. 15:1-9)* When the Lord sent Saul to destroy Amalek, he spared the king and the best cattle.

## The United Kingdom

Saul went downhill spiritually until he ended up going to see the Witch of Endor so that he might talk with the deceased Samuel.

*The Rejection of Saul (1 Sam. 15:10-35)* Because Saul failed to obey, God sent Samuel to denounce Saul's wickedness: "You have rejected the word of the Lord and the Lord has rejected you from being king over Israel" (1 Sam. 15:26). Ultimately, Saul died by his own hand on the slopes of Mt. Gilboa.

## The Reign of David

With David, who ruled from 1011 BC to 971 BC, comes the most glorious era in the history of Israel. More is known about him than any other man in Israel's history. In 1993, a stele was discovered at the site of the ancient city of Dan. It is the record of the conquest of one of the kings of Aram sometime during the ninth century BC. It contains the first reference found outside the Bible to the "House of David." There is now archaeological proof of the existence of David.

*Shepherd (1 Sam. 16:1-17:58)* Little of David's early life is known. He kept his father's flock around Bethlehem. On one occasion, he slew a lion and a bear. Then, he took on and was victorious over t he giant Goliath.

*Courtier (1 Sam. 18:1-19:24)* Saul called David to live at the court. David became the captain of the king's bodyguard, a position second only to Abner, the army general.

*Fugitive (1 Sam. 20:1-31:13)* Saul soon became jealous. David was driven from the court and, for several years, became a fugitive.

As he recorded in the Psalms again and again, he narrowly escaped death.

*King (2 Sam. 1:1-10:19)* When Saul died, the tribe of Judah made David king. David was a man after God's heart (1 Sam. 13:14; Acts 13:22). After reigning for seven years in Hebron over Judah, the other tribes chose David as their king. David then moved the capital from Hebron to Jerusalem.

David captured Jerusalem when Joab climbed up a "water shaft" (2 Sam. 5:6-9; 1 Chron. 11:4-7). In 1867, General Sir Charles Warren, an officer in the British Royal Engineers, and his assistant discovered and explored a shaft in Jerusalem named "Warren's Shaft." The Hebrew word translated "water shaft" is a rare word whose meaning has been debated. The use of this word in the only other passage where it appears in the Old Testament ("waterfalls" in Ps. 42:6) and the use of a related word ("pipes" in Zech. 4:12) support the rendering of the water shaft in 2 Samuel 5:8.

For the next thirty-three years, David ruled over Israel. He was used as the standard for all the rest of the kings. The Lord told David: "When your days are fulfilled and you rest with your fathers, I will set up your seed after you, who will come from your body, and I will establish his kingdom. He shall build a house for My name, and I will establish the throne of his kingdom forever" (2 Sam. 7:12-13).

Israel wanted a king and God gave them one, but the will of God was for an eternal kingdom ruled over by the Son of David, namely, God's Son, Jesus Christ. God promised Abraham a land and descendants who would bless the world. Now, He promises

## The United Kingdom

David, a descendant of Abraham, that his descendant will establish an eternal kingdom.

*Transgressor (2 Sam. 11:1-24:25)* David committed adultery with Bathsheba and had her husband killed. As a result, even though David repented, he had trouble in his family and in the kingdom.

## The Reign of Solomon

Solomon, the son of David, succeeded his father as king from AD 971 to AD 93.

*The Wisdom of Solomon (1 Kings 1:1-4:34)* Solomon came to the throne at an early age, perhaps as young as twenty. One of the first things he did was to call an assembly at Gibeon, the location of the Tabernacle. He offered a thousand burnt offerings. When God asked him what he wanted, Solomon asked for wisdom. Because Solomon requested wisdom rather than riches, honor, longevity of life, or the life of his enemies, God was pleased and declared that he would have all of those as well as wisdom. Solomon ruled wisely. He completed and perfected the policies begun by his father, David.

*The Buildings of Solomon (1 Kings 5:1-8:66)* Solomon built a Temple, a palace, and carried on an extensive building program in Jerusalem and throughout the kingdom. First Kings 7:12 says Solomon used a construction consisting of "three rows of hewn stone and a row of cedar beams." This type of construction has been found at Megiddo.

## A Plane View of The Bible

*The Disobedience of Solomon (1 Kings 9:1-11:43)* The Scripture specifically says that Solomon refortified the cities of "Hazor, Megiddo, and Gezer" (1 Kings 9:15). The gates of these three cities have been excavated. All three are six-chambered gates connected to a double wall. They are virtually identical. They have similar dimensions and are built on the same plan.

Amnon Ben-Tor, a Jewish archeologist, has concluded that the gate and wall at Hazor were built in the tenth century BC, about 950 BC. He does not want to attribute the gate and wall to Solomon. He says that is not an archaeological conclusion but the job of a historian or Bible scholar. He does say, "There is no reason why the gate and the casemate wall could not be attributed to King Solomon." He even calls it "likely."

William G. Dever, an American archaeologist who excavated at Gezer, argues that someone built the three gates at Gezer, Megiddo, and Hazor "in a highly centralized government," and that "means statehood." He dates the gates to the tenth century BC and adds, "If Solomon hadn't lived, we would have to invent a Solomon by another name to account for the archeological evidence." I have heard Dr. Dever lecture (with slides) on the identical design of the gates, indicating that there was central control, a state. It was impressive.

First Kings says, "Pharaoh King of Egypt had gone up and taken Gezer and burned it with fire, had killed the Canaanites who dwelt in the city and had given it as a dowry to his daughter, Solomon's wife" (1 Kings 9:16). At Gezer, archaeologists found a massive layer of ash that covered most of the mound. In it were

## The United Kingdom

Hebrew, Egyptian, and Philistine artifacts, indicating that all three cultures had been there simultaneously, which is exactly what the Bible says.

The queen of Sheba came to see Solomon (1 Kings 10:1-10). Cuneiform sources have verified that she was head of a tribal confederacy in southern Arabia.

First Kings says Solomon collected thousands of horses "whom he stationed in the chariot cities" (1 Kings 10:26-29). Excavations at Megiddo also uncovered two stable compounds holding about 450 horses. Some say these are from Solomon's time, although others contend that they were from the period of Ahab (9th cent. BC).

After the custom of the oriental kings, Solomon made alliances with foreign nations and married the daughters of these foreign rulers, including the daughter of Pharaoh. Thus, he established an extensive harem. These women brought in their gods and turned the heart of Solomon from the worship of the Lord. The usual forms of sacrifice and worship were maintained, but the spirit was not in those forms. The Lord told Solomon, "Because you have done this, and have not kept My covenant and My statutes, which I have commanded you, I will surely tear the kingdom away from you and give it to your servant" (1 Kings 11:11).

**Summary:** During the United Kingdom, a king was established in Israel, and three men ruled over the nation, each for forty years.

Israel wanted a king, so God gave them a king and a kingdom. He also used this time to promise the establishment of an eternal kingdom, one in which the Son of David, God's Son Jesus Christ, will rule forever (2 Sam. 7:12-13).

Many accomplishments occurred during this "golden age" of Israel's history. Many books of Scripture were written: Judges, Ruth, 1 and 2 Samuel, Ecclesiastes, the Song of Solomon, most of the Psalms, and Proverbs. The Temple was built and dedicated. Sacred music was introduced. Under David and Solomon, the kingdom expanded, consisting of about six times as much territory as was initially occupied by the twelve tribes.

The spiritual lesson to be learned from this period is that even the best of men have faults and failures; only God Himself is perfect and capable of ruling perfectly. Physically, Saul was head and shoulders above everyone else (1 Sam. 10:23). Spiritually, David had a desire for the Lord as great as or greater than anyone did (Ps. 42:1; Acts 13:22). Mentally, Solomon was wiser than all others were (1 Kings 4: 29-34). Yet all three had faults and failed one way or another to do God's will. A greater than Saul, David and Solomon is needed to rule in God's kingdom

Chapter 5

# THE DIVIDED KINGDOM

The period of the Divided Kingdom began in 931 BC with the death of Solomon and the division of the kingdom. For 209 years, the two kingdoms stood side by side. In 722 BC, Assyria conquered the Northern Kingdom, carrying away many. The Southern Kingdom existed alone until 605 BC when Nebuchadnezzar of Babylon defeated Jerusalem.

## The Two Kingdoms

For David's sake, the Lord deferred the division of the kingdom until after Solomon's death, but the kingdom was divided under Solomon's son, Rehoboam. There were several causes. First, there had been a rivalry between the tribes of Ephraim and Judah since the time of Joshua. During the latter years of Saul's reign, Ephraim supported Saul while Judah rallied around David. After the influences of David and Solomon passed off the scene, the old feelings arose again. Also, when Solomon disobeyed the Lord and his heart was turned toward other gods, the Lord decreed the dissolution of the kingdom. The catalyst was Rehoboam's folly. The kings had become wealthy, but the people were financially oppressed. When they assembled at Shechem and pleaded for taxes to be reduced, Rehoboam (taking the advice of young peers instead of the elders) answered, "My little finger shall be thicker than my father's loins" (1 Kings 12:10). As a result, the northern tribes revolted; the kingdom was split into two nations.

The Northern Kingdom, called Israel, consisted of ten tribes. The Southern Kingdom, known as Judah, only had two. The Northern Kingdom contained over 9,500 square miles, while Judah comprised 3,500 square miles. The land of the Northern Kingdom was more productive. The Southern Kingdom had Jerusalem, the site of the Temple.

The relationship between the two kingdoms varied. At first, there was a period of hostility lasting sixty years. During this time, Rehoboam and his successors persisted in an unsuccessful effort to subdue Israel. Then, for thirty years, there was a period of alliance. The alliance was between Ahab in the North and Jehoshaphat in the South against foreign foes. After that, there was a period of renewed hostility, which lasted 169 years. When Jehu came to the throne of Israel, he severed the ties between the two kingdoms. From that time on, there was ceaseless strife between the North and the South.

## The Northern Kingdom

All nineteen kings of the Northern Kingdom were wicked. Significant kings and the prophets of the Northern Kingdom are as follows.

## The Divided Kingdom

### Kings

*Jeroboam (1 Kings 12:1-14:21)* Jeroboam introduced idolatry into the Northern Kingdom. Believing that if his people in the North traveled to Jerusalem to worship, his kingdom would be threatened, Jeroboam set up idol worship in Dan, an extreme northern city, and Bethel, situated on the border between Israel and Judah. "Therefore, the king took counsel and made two calves of gold, and said to the people, 'It is too much for you to go up to Jerusalem. Here are your gods, O Israel, which brought you up from the land of Egypt!'" (1 Kings 12:28).

Throughout the history of the Northern Kingdom, references are made to the fact that the kings who came after Jeroboam did evil in the sight of the Lord by walking in the way of Jeroboam. His sin was the root cause of Israel's fall. The "sin of the house of Jeroboam" destroyed Israel "from the face of the earth" (1 Kings 13:34).

The Scripture says that Shishak of Egypt conquered Jerusalem in the fifth year of Rehoboam's reign (1 Kings 14:25). According to Thiele, the date was in 926 or 925 BC. Shishak is the first Pharaoh mentioned by name in the Bible. He is Sheshonk I, the founder of the XXII Dynasty. A triumphal relief at Karnak (ancient Thebes) depicts 156 captives. On the body of each captive appears the name of a place he conquered. About 120 names are legible, but not all of those are identifiable. Among those that can be identified are Megiddo and Gibeon. This indicates that he invaded the Northern Kingdom as well as the Southern Kingdom. The Stele of Shishak dug up at Megiddo, the text of which was published in 1929, indicates that he captured and occupied that city.

*Omri (1 Kings 16:21-28)* Omri purchased the hill of Samaria and built the city of Samaria on it.

In 1868, F. A. Klein, a German missionary, discovered a stone with an inscription in Moab. Hence its name, the Moabite Stone. It is about four feet high and two feet wide with a rounded top. It contains thirty-four lines describing the successful revolt of Mesha, King of Moab, over Israel. It was made *ca.* 850 BC and mentions Omri by name.

In the spring of 1869, Charles Clermont-Ganneau, a French archaeologist who wanted the Moabite Stone for France, had an impression made and offered a large sum for the stone itself. The local Governor demanded an even higher price. Rather than getting nothing for the stone, the native Arabs broke it into pieces and distributed it among different families. Later, many of the pieces were collected, and the stone was pieced back together, but without the impression taken before the stone was broken into pieces, it would have been impossible to restore it.

Today, the restored Moabite Stone is in the Louvre in Paris. Based on the fact that the form of the letters of the Moabite Stone is consistent with other inscriptions of the 9th century BC, archeologists have concluded that it is from that period. Linguistic peculiarities of the period confirm this conclusion.

The Moabite Stone says that Israel conquered and maintained control of the land of Medeba during Omri's reign and half of his son's reign, that is, for 40 years. Then King Mesha revolted, and his god, Chemosh, gave him the victory. There are two possible conflicts with that account and the record: 1) the forty years extend beyond Ahab's death, and 2) Second Kings 3:4-27 says Mesha's revolt was after the death of Ahab. The word translated "son," however, can mean "grandson" or even "descendant." Therefore, there is no conflict between the two accounts. The Moabite Stone is extra confirmation of the existence of Omri. It also contains one of the oldest existing and extra-occurrences of Yahweh as the name of Israel's God. Thus, this stone helps demonstrate the historical accuracy of the Old Testament.

From this time on, in Assyrian records, Israel is mentioned as the "house of Omri."

*Ahab (1 Kings 16:29-22:40)* Ahab, the son of Omri, married Jezebel. They introduced Baal worship into Israel. Elijah confronted this king.

Shalmaneser III, one of the greatest Assyrian kings, left detailed records of his conquest. Several well-preserved monuments have been found. The Monolith Inscription is a large slab with a near-life-size portrait of the king covered with two columns of writing. It gives an account of the battle of Qarqar on the Orontes in 853 BC, a battle not mentioned in the Bible. The inscription credits "Ahab, the Israelite" with having the most powerful military elements in a twelve-state coalition.

First Kings 22:39 says Ahab built an ivory house. Amos prophesied that the houses of ivory in Samaria would perish (Amos 3:15; see also 6:4). As predicted, Samaria was destroyed. When the site was excavated in 1935, fragments of ivory were found spread over the entire city. They were particularly thick near the center of the north city wall, where the ivory house may have been located. Ivory panels in relief were also found.

*Jehu (2 Kings 9:30-10:36)* Jehu slew Jehoram, the king before him, ordered the death of Jezebel, and assembled the priests and the prophets of Baal in the temple (which Ahab had erected in Samaria) and had them slain. His reforms were not long-lasting. Elisha was the prophet during this time.

The Black Obelisk, another of Shalmaneser III's monuments, is a solid block of basalt over six feet high with text and pictures inscribed on all four sides. It was found in 1846 and is now in the British Museum. The Black Obelisk contains an image of Jehu or his ambassador bowing at Shalmaneser's feet and presenting him with gifts. The inscription speaks of tribute from "Jehu, son of Omri." Jehu was only a successor with no lineal relationship to Omri. Thus, "son" is used as a successor. The Scripture does not record Jehu paying tribute to Shalmaneser, but there is no reason to say he did not. At any rate, this is archaeological proof of the existence of Jehu.

*Jehoash (2 Kings 13:10-25)* Second Kings 13:25 says Jehoash recaptured cities "from the hand of Ben-Hadad, the son of Hazael." The Stele of Zakir, found in 1903 in northern Syria, mentions Ben-Hadad II of Aram.

*Jeroboam II (2 Kings 14:23-29)* Jeroboam II kept up the idolatry of the golden calves. Idolatry, drunkenness, and lasciviousness were rampant. Politically, he did much to strengthen and extend the kingdom. Amos and other prophets were sent to denounce the

## The Divided Kingdom

sins of the day and call the people back to the worship of Yahweh.

*Menahem (2 Kings 15:16-22)* Second Kings 15:19 says, "Pul king of Assyria came against the land; and Menahem gave Pul a thousand talents of silver, that his hand might be with him to strengthen the kingdom under his control." This is a classic illustration of critics arguing that archaeology proves that the Bible is wrong, only to have archaeologists later demonstrate that the Bible is right. When Assyrian inscriptions were first discovered, the names of Sennacherib, Shalmaneser, Tiglath-Pileser, and other Assyrian kings were found, but Pul was not. More serious was that his name did not appear in the list of kings and there was no gap in any of the list for his name to be inserted.

Later, however, it was discovered that on one list appears the name Tiglath-Pileser, whereas on another, in the same year, the name Pul is written Pulu. All Assyriologists are now agreed that Tiglath-Pileser and Pul are the same individual. When the Assyrian Tiglath-Pileser became king of Babylon, to avoid offending them, he took the Babylonian name, Pulu. By the way, 1 Chronicles says, "So the God of Israel stirred up the spirit of Pul king of Assyria, that is, Tiglath-Pileser king of Assyria" (1 Chron. 5:26). This is another illustration of the historical accuracy of the Bible.

This event is mentioned in the annals of Tiglath-Pileser III (Pul), which says, "As for Menahem terror overwhelmed him like a bird. Alone, he fled and submitted to me. To his palace, I brought him back and silver, colored woolen garments, linen garments ... I received as his tribute."

Other people mentioned in this section of 2 Kings are named in Assyrian records, including Azariah of Judah (2 Kings 15:1-7), Rezin (Rasunna) of Aram (2 Kings 15:37; 16:5, 6, 9), Ahaz of Judah (2 Kings 16:7-8), Pekah and Hoshea (2 Kings 15:30).

*Hoshea (2 Kings 17:1-41)* Hoshea was the last king of Israel. The Assyrian forces, first under Shalmaneser and later under Sargon, laid siege to Samaria, the capital of Israel. After a three-year struggle, the city was taken in 722 BC. Hoshea and his people were taken captive to Assyria. Second Kings 17:6 says, "The king of Assyria took Samaria" and carried captives to Assyria. In his Khorsabad Annals, Sargon says, "I besieged and captured Samaria carrying off 27,290 of the people who dwelt therein. Fifty chariots I gathered from among them."

**Prophets**

A prophet is a person who receives messages directly from God (Num. 12:6) and speaks for Him. Prophets had existed before in Israel. In fact, Moses was a prophet. The office of prophet, however, began with Samuel, one of the judges. When Saul became king, Samuel became the first "prophet." During the period of the divided Kingdom, the office of prophet became prominent. They were "advisors" to the king.

*Elijah (1 Kings 17:1-19:21)* Elijah ministered during the reign of Ahab, battling against Baal worship. He stopped the rain in Israel, challenged the prophets of Baal on Mt. Carmel and denounced Ahab for the murder of Naboth.

## The Divided Kingdom

*Elisha (2 Kings 4:1-8:15)* His many miracles include 1) the multiplying of oil enabling a prophet's widow to pay her debt, 2) the raising from the dead of a child, 3) the healing of Naaman from his leprosy, 4) making a borrowed ax head to swim, and 5) smiting the Syrian forces with blindness.

*Jonah (2 Kings 14:25; Book of Jonah)* Jonah lived during the reign of Jeroboam II (2 Kings 14:25). Jeroboam II ruled from 782-753 BC, after the time of Elijah and just before the time of Amos and Hosea. So the date of Jonah is 760 BC. Jonah was sent to preach to Nineveh, the capital of Assyria.

Assyria was in a mild decline because of weak rulers, yet she remained a threat and her cruelty was legendary. Conditions at Nineveh, however, prepared it to be receptive to Jonah's message. Under Semiramis, the queen regent and her son Adad-Nirari III (810-782 BC), monotheism was introduced under the worship of the god Nebo. Assyrian history records a plague in 765 BC, a total eclipse on June 15, 763 BC, regarded as an indication of divine wrath, and another plague in 759 BC.

Jonah 3:3 says, "Nineveh was an exceedingly great city, a three-day journey in extent." A day's journey is an ancient expression referring to the distance a traveler could cover in one day. It's not an exact measurement because the countryside and circumstances vary, but it is generally considered to be twenty to thirty miles. Archeologists have extensively excavated Nineveh and have discovered that the city walls were only eight miles in circumference, making the city only three miles in length and less than a mile and a half in breadth. How could Jonah travel a three-day journey into it if it was that small?

The Nineveh in the book of Jonah, had a population of 600,000. Jonah 4:11 says there were 120,000 children. If children made up one-fifth of the city, it had a population of 600,000. Therefore, the book of Jonah must refer to the metropolis of Nineveh. In Genesis 10:11, 12, Rehoboth Ir, Calah, and Resen are listed with Nineveh, a "great" or "principal" city. So Nineveh, including its suburbs, stretched from Khorsabad, about twelve miles northeast of Nineveh proper, to Nimroud (Calah), about fifteen miles southeast of the city. The metropolis was about thirty miles from end to end. It was a journey of more than sixty miles or three days at twenty miles a day.

*Amos (Book of Amos)* Technically, Amos was a herdsman, not a prophet (7:14). He denounced the prevailing sins at Bethel. He predicted the Assyrian captivity when outward prosperity made the prediction seem highly improbable.

*Hosea (Book of Hosea)* Hosea ministered during the reign of Jeroboam II and several other kings. He was a contemporary of Amos. His marriage to a prostitute was used as an illustration of God's love for unfaithful Israel.

## The Southern Kingdom

The Southern Kingdom lasted 135 years longer than the Northern Kingdom because of 1) their greater loyalty to Yahweh, 2) the mercy of God for David's sake, and 3) the influence of the prophets, especially Isaiah and Hezekiah. Eight of their twenty kings were called good.

## Kings

*Rehoboam, Judah's first king (1 Kings 14:21-31)* Rehoboam was a true son of his father, Solomon. He followed the Lord until a large harem surrounded him. Then, "he did evil because he did not prepare his heart to seek the Lord" (2 Chron. 12:14). His folly in dealing with taxes triggered the division of the kingdom.

*Asa (1 Kings 15:9-24)* Asa began by inaugurating religious reforms and seeking to win the hearts of the people to the Lord. Basically, he reigned wisely and well. He did, however, fail to inquire of the Lord and he purchased the assistance of the king of Syria against Israel.

Second Kings 15:18 says that Asa sent silver and gold to "Ben-Hadad, the son of Tabrimmon, the son of Hezron, king of Syria, who dwelt in Damascus." In 1940, the Stele of Ben-Hadad, called the Melqart Stele after Ben-Hadad's god, was discovered in northern Syria. It confirms the dynastic order in 1 Kings 15:18.

*Jehoshaphat (1 Kings 22:41-50)* Jehoshaphat is said to have sought the Lord with all of his heart and to have walked in the first ways of his father, David. He ruled wisely. Under his reign, Judah reached a high degree of prosperity.

*Joash (2 Kings 11:17-12:21)* In his early years, Joash was a reformer, repairing the Temple and re-establishing the worship of the Lord. In his last days, however, he was embroiled in sin and embittered by a painful bodily affliction.

*Azariah (2 Kings 14:21-22, 15:1-7)* Azariah, also known as Uzziah (2 Chron. 26:1-22; Isa. 6:1; etc.), began to reign when he was sixteen and reigned in Jerusalem for fifty-two years. He was faithful to the Lord in his early years. Later, however, his heart was turned away from the Lord, and because he usurped the office of priest and undertook sacrifice, he was smitten with leprosy.

*Hezekiah (2 Kings 18:1-20:21)* Hezekiah was a good king who was the greatest reformer in Israel's history. "He trusted the Lord God of Israel so that after him was none like him among all the kings of Judah, or any who were before him" (2 Kings 18:5).

In the sixth year of Hezekiah's reign, Samaria fell to the Assyrians. Isaiah records, "In the fourteenth year of King Hezekiah ... Sennacherib king of Assyria came up against all the fortified cities of Judah and took them" (Isa. 36:1). He then attacked Jerusalem.

Hezekiah withstood the attack. To supply water during the siege, he dug a tunnel from a pool outside Jerusalem to a pool inside Jerusalem. Second Kings 20:20 (see also 2 Chron. 32:30) says Hezekiah "made a pool and a tunnel and brought water into the city." This tunnel, called Hezekiah's Tunnel, still exists today. It is 1777 feet long and extends from Gihon Spring outside the wall of Jerusalem to the Pool of Siloam inside Jerusalem. In 1880, an inscription was found in the tunnel about nineteen feet from the pool of Siloam.

The inscription, now in a museum in Istanbul, Turkey, contains six lines written in Hebrew that tell how the tunnel was constructed. It says: "Now, this is the story of the boring-through;

while the excavators were still lifting up their picks, each towards his fellow, and while there were yet three cubits to excavate, there was heard the voice of one calling to another, for there was a crevice in the rock on the right hand. And on the day they completed the boring-through, the stonecutters struck pick against pick, one against the other, and the waters flowed from the spring to the pool, a distance of 100 cubits. And a hundred cubits was the height of the rock above the heads of the stonecutters."

Second Kings 18:13-19:37 relates Sennacherib's failure to take Jerusalem. The annals of Sennacherib preserved on the Taylor Cylinder, now in the British Museum, say, "As for Hezekiah, the Jew, who did not submit to my yoke, forty-six of his strong walled cities as well as the small cities in their neighborhood ... I besieged and took ... himself, like a caged bird, I shut up in Jerusalem, his royal city." In other words, Sennacherib plays up his successes, but his statement proves that he did not capture Jerusalem. This took place in 701 BC.

By the way, Isaiah says, "So Sennacherib king of Assyria departed and went away, returned home, and remained at Nineveh. Now it came to pass, as he was worshiping in the house of Nisroch, his god, that his sons Adrammelech and Sharezer struck him down with the sword, and they escaped into the land of Ararat. Then Esarhaddon, his son, reigned in his place" (Isa. 37:37-38).

Isaiah has been proven to be accurate. Archaeologists have found writings of Esarhaddon that contain these words: "A firm determination fell upon my brothers. They forsook the gods and turned to their deeds of violence, plotting evil.... My brothers...to gain the kingship, they slew Sennacherib, their father."

*Manasseh (2 Kings 21:1-18)* Manasseh, the son of Hezekiah (one of Judah's best kings), was the worst. He brought back the idolatry his father had destroyed. "He seduced them (Israel) to do more evil than the nations whom the Lord had destroyed before the children of Israel" (2 Kings 21:9). Israel never fully recovered from his wickedness.

Manasseh is mentioned twice in Assyrian records. He is listed as one of the kings who provided materials for the palace of Esarhaddon, the Assyrian king. Later, he is listed as one of the kings who paid tribute to Ashurbanipal. An Assyrian monument mentions his visit to Nineveh (2 Chron. 33:10-13).

*Josiah (2 Kings 22:1-23:30)* Josiah did "that which was right in the sight of the Lord." He thoroughly purified the land from idol worship and undertook the repair and beautification of the Temple, which had been neglected for many years. A copy of the Law was found during the remodeling, and a revival resulted.

*Jehoiakim (2 Kings 23:34-37)* Jehoahaz, a son of Josiah, succeeded his father and reign for three months when Pharaoh Necho put him in prison. He died in Egypt. Necho put Eliakim, another son of Josiah, on the throne and changed his name to Jehoiakim. In 605 BC, Nebuchadnezzar defeated Necho in the Battle of Carchemish and conquered Jerusalem. He took a number of the inhabitants captive to Babylon, including Daniel and his three friends.

*Jehoiachin (*a.k.a. *Jeconiah and Coniah; 2 Kings 24:1-16).* Jehoiachin, the son of Jehoiakim, was king on Saturday, March

## The Divided Kingdom

16, 597 BC (Thiele's date), when Nebuchadnezzar again captured Jerusalem and carried another group captive to Babylon, including Ezekiel and Jehoiachin (2 Kings 24:15). Tablets found near the famous Ishtar Gate in Babylon, dating between 595-570 BC, include the name of Jehoiachin as well as many Jewish names similar to those in the Old Testament.

The Babylonian records say Nebuchadnezzar "seized the city and captured the king. He appointed there a king of his own heart (see Zedekiah below), received its heavy tribute and sent them to Babylon."

*Zedekiah (2 Kings 24:17-25:21)* Second Kings 24:17 says, "Then the king of Babylon made Mattaniah, Jehoiachin's uncle, king in his place, and changed his name to Zedekiah." Zedekiah was the last king of the Southern Kingdom. Jerusalem was destroyed on July 18, 586 BC (Thiele's date), and Zedekiah was carried captive to Babylon. There were three conquests and three deportations.

Second Kings 25:23 says that the king of Babylon made Gedaliah the governor. A seal impression found at Lachish in 1935 has an inscription that reads, "to Gedaliah who is over the household." The title "who is over the house" was used by the chief administrative official next in rank to the king.

**Prophets**

*Obadiah (Book of Obadiah)* Obadiah (*ca.* 850 BC) was written to Israel but is about judgment on Edom. Without using its name, Obadiah graphically describes the almost impregnable fortress of

Petra, the rose-red city carved into the hills high in the mountains with only one very narrow passage into it.

*Joel (Book of Joel)* During the reign of Joash (835-796 BC), Joel used a locust plague as a sign of judgment from God on sin.

*Micah (Book of Micah)* Micah, a contemporary of Isaiah, predicted the Assyrian captivity, which was fulfilled in his day. He also predicted the destruction of Judah and the Babylonian captivity and that the Messiah would be born in Bethlehem (Micah 5:2).

*Isaiah (Book of Isaiah)* Isaiah prophesied during the last year of the reign of Azariah (Uzziah, 790-739 BC) and continued through the reign of Jotham (750-731 BC), Ahab (735-715 BC) and Hezekiah 715-686 BC). Isaiah was an eloquent prophet who influenced the court. He prophesied the virgin birth of Jesus (Isa. 7:14) and described the crucifixion (Isa. 53:1-12). Many consider him to be the greatest of all the prophets.

In 1947, two shepherds found elongated jars in the Qumran area near the Dead Sea. Inside were decaying rolls of leather. Among other manuscripts was an exceptionally well-preserved complete copy of Isaiah. After examining a print of part of Isaiah, W. F. Albright, the famous archaeologist, declared this to be the "greatest manuscript discovery of modern times." Although there was doubt and debate at first, due to other discoveries in the area, including a Qumran settlement, scholars agree that the scrolls come from 250 BC to just before AD 70. The date of the Isaiah manuscript is about 100 BC. Before the discovery of the Dead Sea Scrolls, the oldest extant copy of Isaiah was from the ninth

## The Divided Kingdom

century AD. With the discovery of the Isaiah manuscript, an extant copy of Isaiah leaped back over a thousand years. Incredible! Isaiah from the Dead Sea Scrolls is virtually identical to the ninth-century copy. The only variations are a few differences between a single and plural word. This discovery indicates that an accurate copy of the Scripture exists today.

Isaiah 20:1 speaks of "Sargon the king of Assyria" sending Tartan against Ashdod. This is the only reference to Sargon in the Bible. For years, critics argued that this was a mistake because no Assyrian king named Sargon was known. Then, his palace of over a hundred rooms was excavated at Khorsabad. Furthermore, his records were discovered. In them, he says, "I besieged ... (and) conquered the cities Ashdod, Gath, Asdu-dimmu." Moreover, archaeologist Moshe Dothan discovered a fragment of an Assyrian stele at Ashdod that says Sargon of Assyria conquered Ashdod. Isaiah has been vindicated!

*Nahum (Book of Nahum)* During the reign of Manasseh (695-642 BC), Nahum predicted the destruction of the Assyrian Empire at least forty years before it happened. His prophecy, which seemed impossible when he gave it, was fulfilled.

*Zephaniah (Book of Zephaniah)* In the reign of Josiah (640-609 BC), Zephaniah vigorously denounced sin.

*Habakkuk (Book of Habakkuk)* Habakkuk, who probably ministered during the reign of Josiah (640-609 BC), questioned God for not judging the sins of Judah and, when told Judah would be judged, objected to God's use of Babylon to do it. God told him that they should just live by faith.

*Jeremiah (Book of Jeremiah)* Jeremiah ministered through the reigns of several kings. He was the last messenger of God concerning the coming judgment on Babylon. Twenty years before the exile, this man, known as the weeping prophet, said the exile would last for seventy years (Jer. 25:12). His prophecies concerning surrounding nations were strikingly fulfilled.

Some inscribed ostraca (pottery shards), the bulk of which can be dated about 589 BC, have been discovered at Lachish. Ostracon III speaks of a certain "prophet." Some scholars claim this is a reference to Jeremiah. Ostracon IV contains a complaint that the *sarim* (notable people) were "weakening the hands" of the people by issuing demoralizing communications. That is the very charge leveled at Jeremiah during the days of Zedekiah (Jer. 38:4).

**Summary:** During the period of the Divided Kingdom, the two Kingdoms of Israel and Judah existed side by side, sometimes in alliance and at other times with hostility. When Israel was conquered, Judah existed alone. Then, the Southern Kingdom was conquered and taken into captivity.

During this period, Assyria became the dominant nation in the world and conquered the North Kingdom. For a concise summary of the history of Assyria, see the appendix.

While there were exceptions, this period was marked by unfaithfulness to the Lord and idolatry, ultimately destroying both Kingdoms.

The overwhelming spiritual point of this period is that sin not only leads to defeat, it leads to destruction! During the period of the Judges, sin led to defeat and servitude. During the period of the Divided Kingdom, idolatry led to destruction.

The Divided Kingdom

## The Chronology of The Divided Kingdom

The Kingdom was divided in 931 BC. There are difficulties in the chronology of the period and apparent discrepancies. Overlapping reigns and parts of years as years can explain these difficulties. Thiele's dates for the period are as follows:

| Kings of Israel | | Kings of Judah | |
|---|---|---|---|
| Jeroboam | 930-909 | Rehoboam | 930-913 |
| Nadab | 909-908 | Abijah | 913-910 |
| Baasha | 908-886 | Asa | 910-869 |
| Elah | 886-885 | | |
| Zimri | 885 | | |
| Omri | 885-874 | | |
| Ahab | 874-853 | Jehoshaphat | 872-848 |
| Ahaziah | 853-852 | Jehoram | 853-841 |
| Joram | 852-841 | Ahaziah | 841 |
| Jehu | 841-814 | Athaliah | 841-835 |
| Jehoahaz | 814-798 | Joash | 835-796 |
| Joash | 798-782 | Amaziah | 796-767 |
| Jeroboam II | 793-753 | Uzziah | 792-740 |
| Zechariah | 753 | Jotham | 750-732 |
| Shallum | 752 | | |
| Menahem | 752-742 | | |
| Pekahiah | 752-732 | Ahaz | 735-715 |

*A Plane View of The Bible*

| | | | |
|---|---|---|---|
| Pekah | 742-740 | | |
| Hoshea | 732-723 | Hezekiah | 715-686 |
| | | Manasseh | 697-642 |
| | | Amon | 642-640 |
| | | Josiah | 640-609 |
| | | Jehoahaz | 609 |
| | | Jehoiakim | 609-598 |
| | | Jehoiachin | 598-597 |
| | | Zedekiah | 597-586 |

*The Divided Kingdom*

## The Spirituality of The Kings

The spirituality of the kings varied from very good to very bad. Some bad kings were partly good, and some good kings were partly bad. Some walked with the Lord, and some served idols. A few were reformers. Despite the repeated warnings of the Prophets, both kingdoms sank lower and lower into idolatry until there was no remedy.

| **Kings of Israel** | | | **Kings of Judah** | | |
|---|---|---|---|---|---|
| Jeroboam | 22 years | Bad | Rehoboam | 17 years | Mostly bad |
| Nadab | 2 years | Bad | Abijah | 3 years | Mostly bad |
| Baasha | 24 years | Bad | Asa | 41 years | Good |
| Elah | 2 years | Bad | Jehoshaphat | 25 years | Good |
| Zimri | 7 days | Bad | Jehoram | 8 years | Bad |
| Omri | 12 years | Extra bad | Ahaziah | 1 year | Bad |
| Ahab | 22 years | The worst | Athaliah | 6 years | Devilish |
| Ahaziah | 2 years | Bad | Joash | 40 years | Good |
| Joram | 12 years | Mostly bad | Amaziah | 29 years | Good |
| Jehu | 28 years | Mostly bad | Uzziah | 52 years | Good |
| Jehoahaz | 17 years | Bad | Jotham | 16 years | Good |
| Joash | 16 years | Bad | Ahaz | 16 years | Wicked |
| Jeroboam II | 41 years | Bad | Hezekiah | 29 years | The best |
| Zechariah | 6 mouths | Bad | Manasseh | 55 years | The worst |
| Shallum | 1 month | Bad | Amon | 2 years | Very bad |

## A Plane View of The Bible

| | | | | | | |
|---|---|---|---|---|---|---|
| Menahem | 10 years | Bad | | Josiah | 31 years | Very good |
| Pekahiah | 2 years | Bad | | Jehoahaz | 3 months | Bad |
| Pekah | 20 years | Bad | | Jehoiakim | 11 years | Wicked |
| Hoshea | 9 years | Bad | | Jehoiachin | 3 months | Bad |
| | | | | Zedekiah | 11 years | Bad |

Chapter 7

# THE CAPTIVITY

When Nebuchadnezzar conquered Jerusalem, he carried captives back to Babylon. Speaking of Nebuchadnezzar (2 Kings 24:11), the Scripture says: "And he carried Jehoiachin captive to Babylon. The king's mother, the king's wives, his officers, and the mighty of the land he carried into captivity from Jerusalem to Babylon" (2 Kings 24:15).

Thus, the place of Captivity was Babylon. There is proof of the exile in Babylon outside the Bible. Tablets found near the famous Ishtar Gate in Babylon, dating between 595-570 BC, include the name of Jehoiachin as well as many Jewish names similar to those in the Old Testament.

As prophesied by Jeremiah, the Captivity lasted for 70 years (Jer. 25:12, 29:10), beginning with the conquest of Jerusalem by Nebuchadnezzar in 605 BC and ending with the beginning of the rebuilding of the Temple under Zerubbabel in 536 BC.

## The Cause

The immediate occasion for the fall of the Southern Kingdom was when kings resorted to political expediency and conquest by strong nations. The actual cause of the Captivity was the sin of Judah's kings and people. The Lord's purpose in allowing the Captivity was to punish their apostasy and to discipline His people.

## The Conditions

The Jews who were carried away captive there were not in slavery. In a sense, they were colonialists. They were permitted freedom in social customs, religion, and commerce. While in captivity, many became wealthy, and some, like Daniel, Mordecai, and Nehemiah, obtained positions in the king's court.

The two major prophets of this period were Daniel and Ezekiel. Daniel ministered in the palace, while Ezekiel ministered among the people.

Daniel was a teenager when he was taken to Babylon in 605 BC. He served in the royal court of Babylon and later, when Persia conquered Babylon, in the court of Persia. Thus, his ministry extended for the entire exile and slightly beyond. He died when he was about ninety years old.

Ezekiel was twenty-five years old when he was deported to Babylon in 597 BC. His wife died in 586 BC, and he probably passed away in about 560 BC. Hence, his ministry lasted approximately twenty-two years.

Nebuchadnezzar boasted about his building in Babylon (Dan. 4:30). German archaeologist Robert Koldewey's excavations, which began in 1899, uncovered the splendor of the ancient city of Babylon, including the Ishtar Gate, the Ziggurat, the Marduk temple, the palace, and the Hanging Gardens. Even bricks with Nebuchadnezzar's name on them have been found.

## The Consequences

The period of the Captivity was not without benefits.

*Monotheism Established* By this experience, the Jews were completely cured of idolatry. From then until now, monotheism has been entrenched among the Jewish people. They never again departed from monotheism.

*Synagogue Developed* When the Jews were out of the land, they were away from the Temple. So, the synagogue, which had not been known before, was established as a religious educational institution. The Mosaic Law became widely known. Unfortunately, legalism, which characterized the Judaism of New Testament times, also developed.

*Messianic Hope Revived* As a result of the captivity, the hope of the coming Messiah was revived. The hearts of the people turned to the prophecies of the Coming One in whom their national hope would be realized.

**Summary:** God took the Southern Kingdom into captivity in Babylon to cure them once and for all of idolatry.

Having conquered Egypt and Assyria during this period, Babylon ruled the world. For a condensed chronicle of Babylon's history, see the appendix.

Disobedience demands discipline. The captivity cured Israel of idolatry. Nevertheless, at this point, they are out of the land. They need to be restored to it.

Chapter 8

# THE RESTORATION

Twice, Jeremiah predicted that the captivity would last 70 years (Jer. 25:11; 29:10). The prophets Isaiah, Jeremiah, and Ezekiel predicted Israel's return to their homeland. The immediate occasion for the return was the defeat of Babylon and the reign of Cyrus, the king of Persia.

Babylon fell on October 12, 539 BC. According to Daniel 5, "Belshazzar, king of the Chaldeans" (Dan. 5:30) was killed the night Babylon fell to "Darius the Mede." Babylonian records, however, do not mention Belshazzar and list Nabonidus as the king of Babylon. Critics used that to say the Scripture is in error in saying Belshazzar succeeded Nebuchadnezzar as king. Then in 1853, an inscription found at Ur revealed that Nabonidus was away in Arabia the night Babylon fell and that he "entrusted the kingship" to Belshazzar, his oldest son, before he left. In other words, father and son were co-regents. This confirms Daniel 5:30, 7:1, etc.

The identity of Darius the Mede is uncertain. No one by that name is known from secular history. Furthermore, it is well established that Cyrus captured Babylon and ruled for nine years. According to the Nabonidus Chronicle, however, Cyrus was not with the army the night Babylon fell. He did not arrive until 18 days later. He had appointed Gubaru to rule in his absence. Several possible solutions have been suggested. Darius the Mede was Cyrus (Wiseman), Gubaru (Whitcomb), or Cambyses, the son of Cyrus, who served under his father as ruler over Babylon and later succeeded him as emperor (Boutflower). Both Daniel and other sources indicate that an official took over in Babylon. Ancient rulers often took other names for themselves. So, these accounts are not in conflict. It is just not certain which individual was Darius.

Babylon was the strongest city in the ancient world at the time. A moat and two walls surrounded the city. There was enough food and water inside the city to last for years. No one had ever defeated it and no one believed it could be defeated. How, then, did Babylon fall? Two ancient authors, Herodotus and Xenophon, report that the conquering troops entered the city by diverting the Euphrates River, which ran through the city, and entered the opening. They found the people in a drunken festival, just like Daniel 5 says.

The restoration of Israel to their homeland began in 536 BC, with the rebuilding of the Temple as a result of the decree of Cyrus, the founder of the Persian Empire, and ended around 400 BC.

## Under Zerubbabel

*The Decree of Cyrus (Ezra 1:1-11)* Ezra 1 says Cyrus made a proclamation to allow the Jews to return to their land. "Now in

*The Restoration*

the first year of Cyrus king of Persia, that the word of the LORD by the mouth of Jeremiah might be fulfilled, the LORD stirred up the spirit of Cyrus king of Persia, so that he made a proclamation throughout all his kingdom, and also put it in writing, saying, Thus, says Cyrus king of Persia: All the kingdoms of the earth the LORD God of heaven has given me. And He has commanded me to build Him a house in Jerusalem, which is in Judah. Who is among you of all His people? May his God be with him, and let him go up to Jerusalem, which is in Judah, and build the house of the LORD God of Israel (He is God) in Jerusalem. And whoever is left in any place where he dwells, let the men of his place help him with silver and gold, with goods and livestock, besides the freewill offerings for the house of God which is in Jerusalem" (Ezra 1:1-4).

The predecessors of Cyrus had sought to remove conquered people from their country. He restored them to their homeland and allowed them to reestablish their national life. The Cyrus Cylinder, discovered by the Assyrian explorer Hormuzd Rassam, tells of Cyrus' restoration policy. One line states, "I gathered together all their populations and restored their dwelling places."

*The Census of the Returnees (Ezra 2:1-70)* Zerubbabel was a prince, a descendant of David. In 536 BC, he led 42,500 Israelites back to Jerusalem. Those who returned gave "freely" (Ezra 2:68) and "according to their ability" (Ezra 6:69) to rebuild the Temple. Ezra says they gave money called "drachmas" (Ezra 2:69), a type of money shown to be authentic for this period.

*The Rebuilding of the Temple (Ezra 3:1-6:22)* Once in the land, they laid the foundation of the Temple, but the nations in and around Judah prevented them from completing the job. So, the work ceased for fourteen years.

During this time, the prophets Haggai and Zechariah ministered. Haggai encouraged the people to undertake the completion of the Temple. Zechariah joined him. In four years, the work was completed. This, the second Temple, was finished in 516 BC. It lacked the magnificence of the former Temple, but the Temple had been restored.

Ezra 4:10 speaks of a Persian king named Osnapper who completed the transplanting begun by Esarhaddon (Ezra 4:1-2). Osnapper is the name for Ashurbanipal (668-626 BC). His palace and royal library of 22,000 volumes, including a collection of creation and flood epics, was found at Kouyunjik.

## Under Ezra

Between Ezra 6 and Ezra 7 is approximately 60 years. Cyrus (Ezra 1:1) and Darius (Ezra 6:1) had passed off the scene. Artaxerxes now sat on the throne.

*The Decree of Artaxerxes (Ezra 7:1-28)* In 458 BC, Ezra secured the authority of the Persian king, Artaxerxes, to take an additional group from Babylon to Jerusalem.

*The Return of Ezra (Ezra 8:1-10:44)* When he arrived, he found the Law was being neglected, intermarriage with pagan nations prevailed and the poor were opposed. Ezra undertook to reform these wrongs.

## Under Nehemiah

*Rebuilding of the Wall (Neh. 1:1-6:19)* In 445 BC, Nehemiah, a Persian court high officer, learned of Jerusalem's conditions. The walls around Jerusalem were broken down and the people were in distress. Nehemiah secured permission from Artaxerxes, the same Persian King who permitted Ezra to return (Ezra 7:1), to return to Jerusalem.

When he arrived, Nehemiah was opposed by Sanballat and Tobiah (Neh. 2:19). Sanballat is mentioned in the Elephantine Papyri in the same letter that refers to Jehohanan (see the next section). In 1962, papyri containing the name of Sanballat were discovered in a cave northwest of Jericho. Archeologists have concluded that perhaps this is a reference to the grandson of the governor of Samaria in Nehemiah's day. The name of Tobiah has been found on the face of a cliff in Jordan (Neh. 2:19 says that Tobiah was an Ammonite!) and has been dated by archaeologist Benjamin Mazar *ca.* the $6^{th}$ or $5^{th}$ century BC (Albright dates it to the $3^{rd}$ century BC). Eight silver vessels from the Persian period were found in the east Delta of Egypt. Three were inscribed. One dish contains the inscription "What Qaynu son of Geshem, King of Qedar, brought (as offering) to (the goddess) Han-Ilat."

In fifty-two days, the repair of the wall was completed. Kenyon's excavation in 1966 revealed that in Nehemiah's day, the perimeter of the wall around Jerusalem had been reduced to about

8500 feet, which explains how repairs could be done so quickly. Malachi ministered during that time.

*Restoration of the Community (Neh. 7:1-13:31)* After rebuilding the wall, Nehemiah registered the people, a revival broke out, the wall was dedicated, and Nehemiah instituted reforms. He returned to Persia in 433 BC but came back to Jerusalem in 420 BC. Malachi ministered in Jerusalem during Nehemiah's absences.

Jehohanan is mentioned in Ezra 10:6 and Nehemiah 12:23. He was a High Priest of Jerusalem. In 1895, the Elephantine Papyri were discovered on an island near Aswan in Upper Egypt. They are from 494-400 BC. These papyri contain legal contracts, deeds, private letters, etc. One was a letter by a Jewish priest at Elephantine to Bagohi, the governor of Judah, requesting financial aid to rebuild the Temple on their island. It mentions Jehohanan, the High Priest of Jerusalem.

**Summary:** During the period of the Restoration, large numbers of Jews returned to Jerusalem. The Temple was rebuilt, the wall was restored, and reforms were instituted.

Persia defeated the Babylonians. Thus, during this period, Persia was the dominant force in the world. For a short synopsis of the history of Persia, see the appendix.

The spiritual truth from this period is that God is faithful to His promises (Ezra 1:1-2). In this case, He promised to restore and He did.

*The Restoration*

## Betweem The Testaments

During the 400 years between the Testaments, several nations ruled Israel.
 1. Israel remained under Persian rule until 331 BC.
 2. The Greeks ruled Israel from 331 to 167 BC. During this period, the Greek language became widely used among the Jews. The Septuagint, a translation of the Old Testament from Hebrew into Greek, was completed.

Greece proper is the southern extremity of the Balkan Peninsula, consisting of two provinces, Peloponnesus and Achaia. Southern Greece (Peloponnesus) is connected to central Greece by a four-mile-long narrow isthmus. (In 1893, a canal was cut through the entire four miles.) Sparta and Corinth are in Southern Greece. Athens is in central Greece. The Romans included the two provinces to the north, Epirus and Macedonia, in the term Greece. Herodotus said that Greece, more than any other country, possessed the most happily tempered seasons. Aristotle felt that the absence of extremes in heat and cold was favorable for intelligence and energy.

The history of Greece can be divided into four parts: 1) **Early History** (1900-759 BC). Few written records from this period exist. Troy was at its height from 1900 to *ca.* 1300 BC. Around 1300 BC, invaders from the north, mostly Dorians, destroyed Greek civilization. About 1020 BC, a group of Ionians settled in Attica, mainly in Athens. The first Olympic Games were held in 776 BC. The *Iliad* is about the Ionians. Homer wrote the *Iliad* and the *Odyssey* about 750-700 BC. 2) **Archaic Period** (750-500 BC). City-states were formed. For a while, Sparta was the most powerful city-state. During the later part of this period, Persia invaded Greece. 3) **Classical Period** (500-332 BC). Though the beginning of this period involved wars, it is still considered the classical period of Greek history. Interest in art, architecture, literature, philosophy, and politics flourished during this period. In 490 BC, Athens defeated the Persians at Marathon, but in 480, Xerxes destroyed Athens. The first Peloponnesian Wars between Sparta and Athens resulted in Sparta defeating Athens (461-446 BC). The second Peloponnesian War between Sparta and Athens again resulted in Athens's defeat (431-405 BC). Socrates lived and taught during the period (469-399 BC), as did Plato (427?-347 BC), Aristotle (384-322 BC), and Hippocrates (460-400 BC). 4) **Hellenistic Period** (332-146 BC). Alexander, the Great of Macedonia, defeated the Persians at Issus in 333 BC. The Persians gave him Egypt and he built Alexandria there. He died in 323 BC. By 146 BC, Rome controlled Greece.

There are only a few references to Greece in the Old Testament. (Dan 8:21, 10:20, 11:2; Joel 3:6; Zech. 9:13). On his missionary journeys, Paul evangelized Macedonia and Greece. Nine Greek cities are mentioned in the New Testament in connection with the ministry of Paul: Amphipolis, Apollonia, Athens, Berea, Cenchreae, Corinth, Neapolis, Philippi, and Thessalonica.

3. In 167 BC, the Jews defeated Antiochus Epiphanes and became independent.

## The Captivity

4. In 63 BC, Pompey conquered Jerusalem, and Israel came under Roman rule. Herod the Great became king in 37 BC and continued until after the birth of Christ.

During the period between the Testaments, the Jewish language, laws, and customs changed so that when the Lord came, conditions differed vastly from those that prevailed about 400 years before, when Nehemiah and Malachi lived and ministered.

Chapter 9

# THE MINISTRY OF CHRIST

The next period of Bible history (and the first period of New Testament history) is popularly called the Life of Christ. A full account of the life of Jesus Christ is not given anywhere inside or outside of the Bible. Instead, Matthew, Mark, Luke, and John record a few details of His life and many details concerning His ministry. Thus, this period should be appropriately named the Ministry of Christ.

With the coming of Jesus Christ, there is a change in the story. In the Old Testament, God promised Abraham a land and descendants who would not only occupy the land but also bless the world. Later, He added the Mosaic Law for the Jewish people to follow. The New Testament says, "For the law was given through Moses, but grace and truth came through Jesus Christ" (Jn. 1:17). Christ fulfilled the Mosaic Law — all of the Law, moral and ceremonial (Mt. 5:17). Therefore, for believers today, the Mosaic Law system has been fulfilled and done away with (2 Cor. 3:7, 11). Believers are not under the Mosaic Law (Rom. 6:14; Gal. 2:19; 4:9-11). That does not mean believers today are without any law whatsoever (1 Cor. 9:21). They are under the Law of Christ

(1 Cor. 9:21), which is the law of love (Gal. 6:2). Love fulfills the law (Rom. 13:8-10; Gal. 5:14).

The period begins before the birth of Christ with the birth and ministry of John the Baptist (*ca.* 6/5 BC). The period concludes with the crucifixion and resurrection of Christ (probably AD 30; some say AD 33). Rome ruled Palestine during this period.

Each Gospel presents a different aspect of Christ's ministry. The material in all four Gospels can be divided into seven parts.

## Preparation

*Bethlehem (Mt. 1:18-25; Lk. 2:1-21)* Mary and Joseph were residents of Nazareth, but they were natives of Bethlehem. When Augustus Caesar decreed that the world should be enrolled in their native towns, Joseph and Mary had to travel to Bethlehem. While there, Mary gave birth to Jesus. Justin Martyr, who died in AD 165, wrote about a tradition of a cave in Bethlehem where Jesus was born. In AD 325, Helena, the mother of Constantine, had a church built over the traditional site. Today, the Church of the Nativity stands on that site. In 1934, William Harvey proved that it dates to only the $6^{th}$ century AD, but he uncovered remains of the Constantinian Church four feet below the present structure.

*Jerusalem (Lk. 2:22-38)* Forty days after the birth of Jesus, in accordance with the law of purification, Mary and Joseph presented Christ in the Temple.

*Bethlehem (Mt. 2:1-12)* Having seen "His" star in the East, the Wise Men (the Magi) came to Jerusalem seeking the newborn

King of Kings. Herod informed them that according to the Scripture, the Messiah was to be born in Bethlehem. The Star directed them to the Christ Child and they offered Him gifts of gold, frankincense and myrrh.

*Egypt (Mt. 2:13-15)* An angel sent Joseph, Mary, and Jesus to Egypt to escape Herod's slaughter of all the male children in Bethlehem two years of age and under.

*Nazareth (Mt. 2:19-23; Lk. 2:39-40)* After the flight to Egypt, Joseph, Mary, and Jesus returned to Nazareth.

*Jerusalem (Lk. 2:41-52)* At the age of twelve, after the Feast of Passover, Jesus astonished the teachers in the Temple.

The Temple that Herod rebuilt and in which Jesus taught had an inscription that forbade Gentiles to enter certain parts of it. One of these famous notices was discovered in perfect condition by Clermont-Ganneau in 1871. It is in the Istanbul Museums. It says, "No Gentile may enter inside the enclosing screen around the Temple. Whoever is caught (entering) is alone responsible for the death (penalty), which follows." Albright says these inscriptions were "probably set up by Herod the Great and were thus standing in the time of Christ and the Apostles."

*Nazareth (Lk. 2:51-52)* After the incident at the age of twelve, nothing more is written about Jesus until He is about thirty years of age, except that He grew up at Nazareth "increasing in wisdom and stature and in favor with God and men" (Lk. 2:51).

*Baptism (Mt. 3:13-17; Mk. 1:9-11; Lk. 3:21-23)* When He was about thirty, Jesus came to John the Baptist at Bethabara to be baptized in the Jordan River. He was baptized "to fulfill all righteousness," that is, that He might be identified with Israel so that He could die for them.

*Temptation (Mt. 4:1-11; Mk. 1:12-13; Lk. 4:1-13)* The Holy Spirit led Jesus to various places, including the wilderness and Jerusalem, where Satan tempted Him. Jesus resisted all the temptations of Satan, quoting Scripture in the process.

*The First Disciples (Jn. 1:35-51)* The first men who began to follow Jesus were John (he is not named in the John passage, but he was one of the two disciples of John the Baptist who followed Jesus; see Jn. 1:35-39), Andrew and Peter, Philip and Nathaniel (a.k.a. Bartholomew).

Bethlehem, Nazareth, Capernaum, Jerusalem, Samaria, Caesarea Philippi, the Sea of Galilee, and other locations are mentioned in the record of the ministry of Christ in the New Testament. There is no question that these places existed during the life of Christ. For example, John 6:23 mentions Tiberias. Excavations began by Gideon Foerster in 1973, which uncovered a gated complex at Tiberias dated to the reign of Herod Antipas, who founded the city and named it in honor of the emperor Tiberius. Any tourist to Jerusalem today can see the ruins of the Pool of Bethesda (Jn. 5:2) and the Pool of Siloam (Jn. 9:7).

## The Early Ministry

*Cana (Jn. 2:1-11)* Accompanied by His first disciples, Jesus went to Cana of Galilee, where they attended a wedding. Jesus performed His first miracle, turning water into wine.

## The Ministry of Christ

*Capernaum (Jn. 2:12)* Apparently, after the experience at Cana, Jesus, His relatives, and His first disciples went to Capernaum for a brief visit. Capernaum was the home of Peter.

*Jerusalem (Jn. 2:13-3:21)* Jesus then traveled to Jerusalem to attend the first Passover of His public ministry. On this occasion, He cleansed the Temple and conversed with Nicodemus. At the end of His conversation with Nicodemus, He uttered those now-famous words: "For God so loved the world that He gave His only begotten Son, that whoever believes in Him should not perish but have everlasting life" (Jn. 3:16).

Eternal life is obtained by believing in Jesus Christ. The word "believe" means "trust." When individuals trust Jesus for eternal life, they are given eternal life *as a gift* (Rom. 6:23). People cannot work their way to heaven; it is a gift (Eph. 2:8-9). It is not obtained by righteous works; it is by God's grace and mercy (Titus 3:5). The Gospel of John was written to teach that the way to have eternal life is by trusting in Jesus Christ (Jn. 20:30-31).

*Aenon (Jn. 3:22-36)* From Jerusalem, the Lord went to an area around the Jordan River and along with John the Baptist, spent several months preaching and healing.

*Sychar (Jn. 4:1-38)* From the southern Jordan area, Jesus traveled north to Galilee, saying He "needed to go through Samaria." At Sychar, He encountered the woman at the well.

## The Galilean Ministry

All four Gospels note that Jesus went to Galilee (Mt. 4:12; Mk.

1:14; Lk. 4:14; Jn. 4:43). Jesus spent the next eighteen months there except for trips to Jerusalem. According to one author, Jesus spoke 52 parables. Another says He uttered approximately 70 parables and parabolic illustrations. He performed 35 miracles. Most of the parables and miracles of Christ recorded in the Gospels took place during the Galilean ministry.

Jesus was rejected at Nazareth, the town of His childhood (Lk. 4:16-30). He then moved to Capernaum (Mt. 4:13), a city on the north end of the Sea of Galilee. He also taught in the Synagogue at Capernaum (Lk. 4:31-36). The current site of a synagogue in Capernaum, dated in the $2^{nd}$ century AD, has been excavated. This is probably the site of the synagogue attended by Jesus. Mark says, "As soon as" they left the synagogue, they entered Peter's house (Mk. 1:29). About thirty feet from the site of the synagogue in Capernaum, the remains of a household church have been found. References by $4^{th}$ to $6^{th}$-century pilgrims and graffiti on the wall indicate that it was built on the site of Peter's house.

While in Capernaum, Jesus also called some of His converts to follow Him so that He might make them fishers of men (Mt. 4:18-22; Mk. 1:16-20; Lk. 5:1-11). Using Capernaum as His headquarters, He made several tours throughout Galilee, periodically going to Jerusalem.

*The First Tour (Mt. 4:23-9:17; Mk. 1:35-2:22; Lk. 4:42-5:39)* On this tour, Jesus healed a leper, instructing him not to tell anyone and show himself to the priest in Jerusalem. Nevertheless, the healed leper told everyone what had happened. As a result, Jesus' notoriety spread rapidly. Returning to Capernaum, the Lord healed a paralytic who was let down through the roof and called Matthew to follow Him.

At this point, Jesus journeyed to Jerusalem, where he healed an invalid man at the pool of Bethesda on the Sabbath. This began a bitter controversy with the Pharisees concerning the Sabbath (Jn. 5:1-47). After a night of prayer, Jesus selected twelve Apostles. He also taught the Sermon on the Mount.

*The Second Tour (Mt. 12:22-50; Mk. 3:19-3:35; Lk. 8:1-21)* When Jesus healed a demon-possessed man and the Pharisees accused Him of doing it by the power of the Devil, Jesus told them that the sin of blasphemy against the Holy Spirit would not be forgiven. After that, Jesus began to speak in parables.

*The Third Tour (Mt. 9:35-11:1; 14:1-12; Mk. 6:6-29; Lk. 9:1-9)* Jesus sent out the Twelve disciples two by two, giving them authority to cast out demons and heal diseases.

Earlier, when John the Baptist was imprisoned, Jesus closed His ministry in Judea and departed for Galilee. Now, John was killed, and Jesus closed his ministry in Galilee.

## The Private Ministry

For the next six months, Jesus focused on training the twelve. On four separate occasions, Jesus and the disciples withdrew from Galilee.

*Across the Sea of Galilee (Mt. 14:13-36; Mk. 6:30-56; Lk. 9:10-17; Jn. 6:1-21)* The Twelve returned and Jesus took them to a "desert place." Nevertheless, a crowd gathered and Jesus miraculously fed them. This miracle is called the Feeding of the 5000. It is the only miracle mentioned in all four Gospels.

*Tyre and Sidon (Mt. 15:21-28; Mk. 7:24-30)* On this trip, a Gentile woman prevailed upon the Lord to heal her daughter.

*Decapolis (Mt. 15:29-38; Mk. 7:31-8:9)* Jesus healed a deaf and dumb man on this trip and fed the 4000.

*Caesarea Philippi (Mt. 16:5-17:23; Mk. 8:13-9:32; Lk. 9:43-45)* Peter made his confession and the Lord was transfigured.

## The Judean Ministry

At the beginning of His ministry, Jesus had spent some time in Judea. Now, toward the end of His ministry, He returned. Only Luke recorded this Judean ministry and only John recorded the Jerusalem visits during this time.

*Jerusalem (Jn. 7:10-10:21)* Jesus forgave the woman caught in adultery and claimed to be the light of the world. He also healed a blind man and gave the Good Shepherd discourse.

*Judea (Lk. 10:1-13:21)* Among other things, Jesus sent out the seventy, gave the parable of the Good Samaritan and denounced the Pharisees.

*Jerusalem (Jn. 10:22-39)* At the Feast of Dedication in Jerusalem, the Jews tried to stone Jesus.

## The Perean Ministry

On two occasions in Jerusalem, the Jews had attempted to stone

## The Ministry of Christ

Jesus (Jn. 8:59, 10:31). After this second attempt, He withdrew from Jerusalem for a short time, probably about three to four months. Although this part of His ministry is often called the Perean ministry because He went to Perea beyond the Jordan River, He also went to other places.

*Perea (Lk. 13:22-17:10; Jn. 10:40-42)* In answer to the complaint that He was receiving and eating with sinners, Jesus gave the parables of the Lost Sheep, the Lost Coin, and the Lost (Prodigal) Son. He told the story of the rich man and Lazarus. He also said: "If anyone comes to Me and does not hate his father and mother, wife and children, brothers and sisters, yes, and his own life also, he cannot be My disciple. And whoever does not bear his cross and come after Me cannot be My disciple. For which of you, intending to build a tower, does not sit down first and count the cost, whether he has enough to finish it; lest, after he has laid the foundation and is not able to finish, all who see it begin to mock him, saying, 'This man began to build and was not able to finish.' Or what king, going to make war against another king, does not sit down first and consider whether he is able with ten thousand to meet him who comes against him with twenty thousand? Or else, while the other is still a great way off, he sends a delegation and asks for conditions of peace. So likewise, whoever of you does not forsake all that he has cannot be My disciple. Salt is good, but how shall it be seasoned if the salt has lost its flavor?" (Lk. 14:26-33).

A disciple is a pupil (the word "disciple" means "learner, pupil."). Eternal Life is by faith "without cost" (see Rom. 3:24, where "freely" means "without cost"). Discipleship, on the other hand, is costly; it costs putting Jesus Christ before every other person (Lk. 14:26), personal purpose (Lk. 14:27) and possessions (Lk. 14:33).

*Judea (Jn. 11:1-54).* At Bethany, a city near Jerusalem, Jesus raised Lazarus from the dead.

*Samaria and Galilee (Lk. 17:11-18:14)* Jesus healed ten lepers on this tour. He also told the parable of the Publican and the Sinner.

*Perea (Mt. 19:1-20:28; Mk 10:1-10:45; Lk. 18:15:30)* Jesus taught about divorce and had a conversation with the rich young ruler.

*Judea (Mt. 20:29-34; Mk 10:46-52; Lk. 18:35-19:28)* Jesus healed Bartimaeus and visited with Zacchaeus.

## The Last Week

As much as twenty-five percent of the Synoptic Gospels (Matthew, Mark, and Luke) and a third of John's Gospel are used to record the last week in the life and ministry of Christ. On Friday, Mary anointed Jesus in Bethany for His burial. On Saturday, He, no doubt, observed the Sabbath.

*Sunday (Mt. 21:1-11; 14-17; Mk. 11:1-11; Lk. 19:29-44)* Jesus rode a donkey into Jerusalem and was hailed as the Messiah. This is called His triumphal entry.

*Monday (Mt. 21:18-19; Mk 11:12-18; Lk. 19:45-48; Jn. 12:20-50)* In the morning, on His way from Bethany to Jerusalem, Jesus cursed a fig tree. Later in the day, He cleansed the Temple.

*Tuesday (Mt. 21:19-26:16; Mk. 11:19-14:11; Lk. 21:37-22:6; Jn. 13:1-20)* This was a busy day. Jesus taught. There was controversy. Jesus delivered the Olivet Discourse. One-tenth of the entire gospel story is devoted to this one day.

*Wednesday* The Gospels do not record what Jesus did on this day.

*Thursday (Mt. 26:17-46; Mk. 14:12-42; Lk. 22:7-46; Jn. 13:1-18:1)* Jesus observed the Passover with the disciples. He instituted the Lord's Supper and delivered the Upper Room Discourse. Later in the night, He prayed in the Garden of Gethsemane.

*Friday (Mt. 26:47-27:66; Mk. 14:43-15:47; Lk. 22:47-23:56; Jn. 18:2-19:42)* Jesus was arrested, endured six trials (before Pontius Pilate and others), was condemned, crucified and buried. An inscription found in Caesarea in 1961 mentions Pontius Pilate. In 1968, physical evidence of a crucifixion was found in an ossuary (a container of bones) in Jerusalem. The ossuary dates to between AD 6 and 66. A crease in the radial bone indicates a nail had been driven through the forearm, not the palm. An iron nail still transfixed the heel bones. The calf bones had been shattered (see Jn. 19:32).

*Sunday (Mt. 28:1-8; Mk. 16:1-8; Lk. 24:1-12; Jn. 20:1-10)* Jesus rose from the dead.

## The Forty Days

After His resurrection and before His ascension, the Lord appeared to various individuals and groups. The Gospels record ten of these appearances.

*The First Day (Mt. 28:9-15; Mk. 16:9-14; Lk. 24:13-43; Jn. 20:11-25)* The Lord appeared five times on the first day: to Mary, to the women, to Peter, to the two on the way to Emmaus, and to the disciples (except Thomas).

*The Next Sunday (Jn. 20:26-31)* One week later, Jesus appeared to the disciples on Sunday evening. This time, Thomas was present.

*Other Appearances (Mt. 28:16-20; Mk. 16:15-18; Lk. 44-49; Jn. 21:1-25; Acts 1:3-8, 1 Cor. 15:6-7)* Later, He appeared to the seven disciples beside the lake, to the 500 on a mount in Galilee, to James, and to the eleven disciples.

*The Ascension (Mk. 16:19-20; Lk. 24:50-53; Acts 1:9-12)* Forty days after His resurrection, the Lord ascended from the Mount of Olives.

**Summary:** Miracles and messages characterized the ministry of Jesus Christ, which culminated in His death, resurrection, appearances, and ascension.

During the life of Christ and the period afterward, Rome ruled the world. For a quick review of Roman history, see the appendix.

The major message of the ministry of Christ is twofold: first, trust Jesus Christ, the One who died for sin and rose from the dead, for the gift of eternal life (Jn. 3:16). Then, become a disciple (a learner) by putting Jesus Christ before every other person (Lk. 14:26), personal purpose (Lk. 14:27) and possessions (Lk. 14:33). The main thing Jesus wants us to learn is to love God and others.

Chapter 10

# THE ACTS OF THE APOSTOLES

This period begins with the descent of the Holy Spirit on the Day of Pentecost (AD 30) and ends with the death of the apostle John (*ca.* AD 95). Although it does not cover the entire time, Acts is this period's main source of information.

## Jerusalem

*The Promise (Acts 1:4-11)* Before He ascended, Jesus promised to send the Holy Spirit. He also told the Apostles to be witnesses. He said: "But you shall receive power when the Holy Spirit has come upon you, and you shall be witnesses to Me in Jerusalem, and in all Judea and Samaria, and to the end of the earth" (Acts 1:8).

Jesus instructed the Apostles to witness concerning Him, that is, preach the gospel, the good news that He died for sin and rose from the dead, starting in Jerusalem and, from there, going to the ends of the earth.

*Pentecost (Acts 2:1-47)* Before His departure, Jesus promised to send the Holy Spirit after He ascended. He instructed the disciples to wait in Jerusalem until the Holy Spirit arrived. They waited ten days until the day of Pentecost. The Holy Spirit came, Peter preached and three thousand were converted.

Pentecost, a word that means fifty, gets its name because it was the day of the Feast of Pentecost (Lev. 23), fifty days after Passover. As Jesus fulfilled the Feast of Passover, the coming of the Holy Spirit fulfilled the Feast of Pentecost. Pentecost can no more be repeated than the crucifixion (or Bethlehem) can be repeated.

*Persecution (Acts 3:1-4:37)* When Peter and John healed a lame man, the Jewish leaders arrested them and forbade them to teach in the name of Jesus Christ. Declaring that they must obey God rather than man, the Apostles continued their work.

*Ananias and Sapphira (Acts 5:1-11)* Believers sold their possessions and put the money into a common fund. Ananias and his wife Sapphira sold their possessions but kept back part of the price. Because of their deception, they fell dead at the word of Peter and great fear fell on the whole church.

*Deacons Elected (Acts 6:1-7)* A conflict arose between the Hellenists (foreign-born Jews) and the Hebrews. The widows of the Hellenists were being discriminated against in the daily distribution of money. The Apostles instructed the church to choose seven men to distribute the money.

*Stephen Martyred (Acts 6:9-7:60)* Stephen, one of the seven chosen to distribute provisions to the widows, performed miracles and preached. The Jewish leaders became so angry at his preaching that they had him stoned.

*The Acts of The Apostoles*

## Judea and Samaria

As a result of persecution, believers were scattered throughout Judea and Samaria, but the Apostles remained in Jerusalem, at least for a time (Acts 8:1-4).

*Samaria (Acts 8:5-40)* Philip, another of the seven chosen to distribute money to the widows, went to Samaria to preach. Many believed. When news of the conversion of the Samaritans reached Jerusalem, Peter and John were sent to Samaria. Under the direction of an angel, Philip left the work in Samaria and went to Gaza, where he shared the gospel with an Ethiopian treasurer. The Ethiopians trusted the Lord and were baptized.

*Damascus (Acts 9:1-31)* A young Pharisee named Saul of Tarsus headed toward Damascus to arrest the disciples of Jesus Christ. As he journeyed, the Lord Himself arrested him. Through the intercession of Barnabas, the disciples at Jerusalem received Saul. He then returned to his native city, Tarsus, where he remained for three or four years until Barnabas came and persuaded him to go to Antioch and aid in the work there.

*Judea (Acts 9:32-10:1-48)* In the meantime, Peter was traveling throughout Judea. During this time, he was called to preach the gospel in Cornelius' household at Caesarea. Cornelius was the first Gentile convert.

## To the End of the Earth

The strong church in Antioch sent Barnabas and Paul on their first missionary journey. Antioch became their headquarters for succeeding trips.

*Paul's First Missionary Journey (Acts 13:1-14:28)* When the Holy Spirit directed Paul and Barnabas to preach the gospel elsewhere, they first sailed to the island of Cyprus, the home of Barnabas. At Pathos, a sorcerer opposed them. Saul, who henceforth would be known as Paul, called down blindness upon the sorcerer. In 2000, it was reported that an inscription reading "Paul Apostle" and dated to the first or second century AD was found on that island.

From Cyprus, they crossed to the mainland, the Roman province of Galatia, known today as Turkey. John Mark left them to return home. They went to Perga and Antioch of Pisidia (not the Antioch from which they first embarked). Driven from Antioch by persecution, they went to Iconium, where they met with a measure of success. From there, they went to Lycaonia, Lystra, and Derbe. Retracing their steps to revisit the people they had led to Christ, they returned to Perga, where they had landed two years earlier. From there, they sailed to Antioch.

After the first missionary journey, Paul wrote the Galatians to the churches of Galatia. Not all scholars agree on the early date of Galatians, but there is no reference in Galatia to the Jerusalem Council. Had it already taken place, this epistle would not have been needed. Therefore, Galatians is the first epistle Paul wrote.

On the first journey, Paul wrote one epistle—Galatians.

*The Council in Jerusalem (Acts 15:1-35)* Once the Gentiles were converted, questions arose concerning how far they should be required to observe the Jewish law. The Apostles and many leaders held a council in Jerusalem to settle the controversy. The council decided that Gentile converts did not have to be circumcised or keep the Mosaic Law.

*Paul's Second Missionary Journey (Acts 15:36-18:22)* As Paul and Barnabas contemplated their second missionary trip, a dispute arose concerning John Mark. Barnabas wanted to take him, but Paul did not. They parted over that issue. John Mark went with Barnabas.

From Antioch, traveling north by land, Paul passed through Syria and Cilicia, confirming the churches established on the first trip. At Lystra, he found Timothy, who became his helper. After spending some time in Galatia, Paul traveled to Troas, where he received the vision of a Macedonian man urging him to spread the gospel in his region.

Paul crossed the Aegean Sea and entered Macedonia. For the first time, the gospel was spreading into Europe. Paul visited Philippi, Thessalonica, Berea, Athens, and Corinth. He labored at Corinth, the chief commercial city of Greece, for a year and a half. After leaving Corinth, he briefly stopped in Ephesus and returned to Antioch.

Luke says, "Claudius had commanded all the Jews to depart from Rome" (Acts 18:2). Suetonius, chief secretary to Hadrian, who reigned from AD 117-138, "confirms" Luke's statements. Suetonius wrote, "As the Jews were making constant disturbances at the instigation of Chrestus, he (Claudius) expelled them from Rome" (Suetonius, *The Life of Claudius*, 25.4).

Also, when Paul was in Corinth, he appeared before the proconsul Gallio (Acts 18:12). An inscription from Delphi, Greece, containing the twenty-sixth acclamation of Emperor Claudius as imperator (that is, the twenty-sixth time Claudius named himself imperator), mentions that Gallio was "proconsul of Achaia." Dating from the twenty-sixth acclamation of Claudius, the inscription is placed between January and August of AD 52. Since Gallio had to have been in office long enough to have made a report and received this commendation, he probably took office in the spring or summer of AD 51. Paul was in Corinth during that time. This is direct proof of the mention of Gallio in Acts.

Paul wrote two epistles on the second journey—1 and 2 Thessalonians.

*Paul's Third Missionary Journey (Acts 18:23-21:15)* On his third missionary journey, Paul retraced the steps he had covered on previous journeys. Starting from Antioch and traveling overland, he went through the regions of Galatia and Phrygia. He eventually reached Ephesus, where he labored for two years and three months. From Ephesus, he passed through Macedonia and again visited Philippi and Corinth. On his return, he stopped at Miletus, the seaport of Ephesus, to deliver a farewell address to the elders. From there, he journeyed through Caesarea and ended up in Jerusalem.

Paul authored three epistles on his third missionary journey: Romans, 1 Corinthians, and 2 Corinthians.

*Journey to Rome (Acts 21:16-28:31)* In Jerusalem, Paul's old enemies, the Jews from Asia, stirred up the people and caused him to be arrested on the unfounded charge that he had brought Greeks into the Temple, defiling the Holy Place. To prevent a plot to kill him, Paul was taken to Caesarea. He remained in prison in Caesarea for two years. Having appealed to Caesar, they transported him to Rome. The book of Acts ends with Paul under house arrest in Rome. He dwelt there for at least two years.

Paul wrote four epistles on his fourth trip: Ephesians, Philippians, Colossians, and Philemon. These are called prison epistles because he wrote them while in prison in Rome. (Paul wrote one epistle on his first trip, two on the second, three on the third, and four on the fourth.)

The cities mentioned in Acts are real cities that existed during the time of the Apostles. These include Jerusalem, Samaria, Damascus, Philippi, Thessalonica, Berea, Athens and Corinth, Ephesus, Caesarea, Rome, etc. Luke names thirty countries, fifty-four cities, and nine islands without an error. Years ago, archaeologist William F. Albright stated, "Most of the cities of Asia Minor and Greece mentioned in the Book of Acts are now securely identified."

*Paul's Ministry Beyond Acts* The book of Acts ends with Paul in prison in Rome. Evidence from tradition seems to indicate that Paul was released from prison and was able to travel again. Perhaps he made it as far as Spain, which had been his dream for some time. Later, he was arrested again and ultimately beheaded in Rome.

Did Paul write five letters on his fifth trip? No. He only wrote three: 1 and 2 Timothy and Titus.

*The Ministry of John* Before AD 70, Paul and Peter were martyred in Rome. In AD 70, Jerusalem was conquered and the Roman general, Titus, destroyed the Temple. For years afterward, until almost the close of the first century, John the Apostle lived and ministered. He wrote the Gospel of John, 1, 2, and 3 John, and Revelation.

**Summary:** After the Holy Spirit came, the Apostles began in Jerusalem and preached the gospels to Rome.

The spiritual truth for the Apostles and for believers today is that God wants the gospel preached starting where they are and from there to the ends of the earth.

# CONCLUSION

One of the best ways to get an overview of the Bible is by seeing its historical periods. A simple summary of those periods is as follows:

| | |
|---|---|
| The Patriarchs | 2167-1806 BC |
| The Exodus | 1527-1407 BC |
| The Conquest | 1407-1400 BC |
| The Judges | 1375-1043 BC |
| The United Kingdom | 1043-931 BC |
| The Divided Kingdom | 931-605 BC |
| The Captivity | 605-536 BC |
| The Restoration | 536-400 BC |
| The Ministry of Christ | 6/5 BC-AD 30 (some say, AD 33) |
| The Acts of the Apostles | 30 (or 33)-AD 95 |

These periods are one way to "outline" the Bible. In terms of an outline, these periods are the "main points" of the outline. The "sub-points" need to be added. For example, the sub-points of the period of the Patriarchs are Abraham, Isaac, and Jacob. To that should be added people, places, customs, events, and spiritual truths revealed during of each of these periods.

As with the outline of any material, knowing the outline does not mean that a person understands the material or the point the material is making. So, while having an outline is helpful, it is only the beginning. As was pointed out in the Introduction, "The Bible was written to teach spiritual truth, that is, to give people knowledge of salvation (2 Tim. 3:15) and to assist believers in growth to spiritual maturity (2 Tim. 3:16-17). Just understanding Bible history, chronology, geography, and customs will not, of course, accomplish any of that. Spiritual birth is by faith (Jn. 3:3, 16), and spiritual growth comes through faith, loving obedience, etc. The ten periods of Bible history will only enable us to understand the Bible's layout."

With an overview of the Bible, you will better understand where you are and what is going on in the text of Scripture. That's good, but it is only the beginning. The object is not to know the text of the Scripture but to know the truth of the Scripture so we can know the God of the Scripture intimately.

*Appendix*

# APPENDIX

During the ten periods of history, other nations rose and fell. Here is a brief summary of the nations that came in contact with Israel.

## MESOPOTAMIA

Mesopotamia was one of the earliest centers of civilization. The word "Mesopotamia" means "land between two rivers." The ancient historian Herodotus named the plains between the Tigris and Euphrates Rivers. Actually, territory on both sides of the rivers was included in the designation. It was about 600 miles long, north to south, with mountains in the north and the Persian Gulf in the South. It was about 300 miles wide, east to west. Today it is roughly the nation of Iraq.

In ancient times, Mesopotamia was divided into two main sections. The northern part was called Assyria. Its main cities, Nineveh, Ashur, and Kharsabad, were all on the Tigris River. The southern section was called Shinar and later Babylon. Its most important cities, Ur, Babylon, etc., were on or near the Euphrates.

Noah's son Ham had a son named Cush (Gen. 10:6). Cush had a son named Nimrod, who went to "the land of Shinar" and built several cities, including Babel (Gen. 10:10). Later, men built a tower at Babel that resulted in the confusion of languages (see Gen. 11:1-9). Still later, it became the well-known city of Babylon. Genesis also says that Nimrod went to Assyria and built cities, including Nineveh (Gen. 10:11-12). Ancient records indicate Sargon I (also called Sargon of Agada, Sargon of Akkad, another name for the city of Agada, and Sargon the Great, who ruled *ca.* 2350-2295 BC, united the Mesopotamia region and is considered by some to be the creator of the first world Empire. He is not mentioned by Sargon in Scripture, but many scholars believe Nimrod was another name for Sargon.

Later, the third Dynasty of Ur ruled much of Mesopotamia until about 2000 BC.

One of the greatest periods of Mesopotamia was between 1830-1550 BC. Hammurabi Babylon (reigned 1792?-1750? BC) was one of the kings during this time.

The Hittites conquered Babylon in about 1595 BC, and the Kassites controlled it for four centuries.

Beginning *ca.* 1350 BC, Assyria began to assert itself, conquering Babylon about 1225 BC. Aramaean and Chaldean tribes overran Babylon.

Assyria reached the peak of its political power between 910-612 BC, conquering Babylon and the world.

The Chaldeans (Babylon) under Nebuchadnezzar II ruled Mesopotamia from 612 until 539 BC. They also conquered the world.

Cyrus the Great of Persia captured Babylon in 539 BC.

After Alexander the Great conquered the region in 331 BC, the Greek dynasty of Seleucus I held Mesopotamia, bringing in

*Appendix*

Hellenistic culture and trade.

About 250 BC, the Parthians took Mesopotamia from the Seleucids. They fell to the Sassanids in AD 224.

Arab tribes conquered the region in AD 635, bringing a new religion, Islam. The Arabic language displaced Greek and even the Persian language. Baghdad became the center of the Islamic Empire under the Abbasid caliphs.

The Ottomans and Safavid Persian rulers vied for control of Mesopotamia from the 16$^{th}$ to the 18$^{th}$ century, with the Turks prevailing. British troops took the area during World War 1 (1914-1918). It became independent in 1932 and Syria in 1945.

## EGYPT

Since the period of the Patriarchs ends with the children of Israel in Egypt and the period of the Exodus begins with their departure from Egypt, an overview of Egyptian history will help put this aspect of history into perspective.

Ancient Egypt consisted of a long, narrow strip of land along the Nile River. From the Mediterranean Sea, it extended about 525 miles south with an average width of twelve miles. It was divided into two parts: 1) Lower Egypt (the Delta region), a pie-shaped area between the Mediterranean Sea and Cairo, measuring about 125 miles north and south and at its greatest width 115 miles east and west. Along the eastern edge of the Delta lay the Land of Goshen, where the children of Israel lived during their 430 years in Egypt. 2) Upper Egypt, the remainder of the country from

Cairo *south* to the first cataract (that is, waterfall), a distance of about 400 miles.

An Egyptian Priest-historian named Manetho wrote a history of Egypt in Greek for Ptolemy I Soter (*ca.* 304-285 BC). He divided Egyptian history into thirty-one dynasties, listing each king and the length of his reign. (A dynasty is the continuous reign of members of the same family or line.) These dynasties were grouped into kingdoms. His outline is the basis for all modern histories of Egypt. His basic work, supplemented with other discoveries, provides the following outline of ancient Egyptian history.

1. The Early Dynastic Period (Dynasties I-II, *ca.* 3100-2800 BC). According to Manetho, the first dynasty began with Menes, who unified Upper and Lower Egypt. Writing was introduced, perhaps from Mesopotamia. The 365-day calendar was invented.

2. The Old Kingdom (Dynasties III-VI *ca.* 2800-2250 BC). Zoser built the first pyramid, the Step Pyramid, at Sakkara. Cheops (Khufu) built the Great Pyramid at Gizeh, one of the seven wonders of the ancient world. It is an engineering marvel. It is almost exactly north and south, east and west. There are 2,300,000 stones in it, weighing an average of 2½ tons each. It is 755 feet square at its base and 492 feet high. Experts estimate that it took 100,000 men 30 years to build it. Chephren (Khafre), Cheops' son, constructed the second pyramid and the Sphinx at Giza. His pyramid was slightly smaller than The Great Pyramid (forty-eight feet less on each side of the base and ten feet less in height). The head of the nearby sphinx probably represents Chephren.

## Appendix

The tomb of Khnumhotep, a noble under Senusret II, depicts 37 Asiatics bringing gifts to Egypt. The inscription reads, "The arrival, bringing eye paint, which 37 Asiatics bring to him." Their leader has a Hebrew name, "Sheik of the highlands Ibahe."

3. First Intermediate Period (Dynasties VII-IX *ca.* 2250-2000 BC). Abraham visited Egypt during this period.

4. Middle Kingdom (Dynasties X-XII *ca.* 2000-1786 BC). Joseph became second only to the Pharaoh (Gen. 41:39-41), probably Senusret II. Later, Jacob and the remainder of the family joined Joseph in Egypt.

5. Second Intermediate Period (Dynasties XIII-XVII *ca.* 1786-1575 BC). The Hyksos ("foreign rulers") conquered Lower Egypt about 1700 BC. A Hyksos ruler was probably the "Pharaoh who did not know Joseph" (Ex. 1:8).

6. The New Kingdom (Dynasties XVIII-XX *ca.* 1575-1085 BC). Ahmose defeated the Hyksos and united Egypt under a new dynasty. During this period, Egypt reached its greatest heights. Thutmose I and Thutmose III marched to the Euphrates. (Thutmose I marched as far as Nahrin, a region beyond the Euphrates.) Tuthmose IV dug the Sphinx out of the sand. Tutankhamun ("King Tut") lived during this period. Later, Ramses II engaged in a massive building program.

Based on the chronology of the Masoretic text (the Hebrew text of the Old Testament), Thutmose III was the Pharaoh of the Oppression, and Amenhotep II was the Pharaoh of the Exodus in 1447 BC. The Egyptians did not record anything uncomplimentary against themselves. So, it is not surprising that nothing has been found that mentions the Exodus.

Merneptah (1224-1216 BC), the successor of Ramses II, has left the first known reference to Israel. He reigned during the time of the Judges. The Merneptah Stone describes his victories. His troubles at home did not allow him to stay in Palestine. So he left Israel at the mercy of the Philistines.

7. Third Intermediate Period (Dynasties XXI-XV *ca.* 1085-663 BC). During this period, the names of Egyptian Pharaohs were first mentioned in the Bible. Sheshonk I ("Shishak") sacked the Temple (927 BC). Assyria invaded Egypt.

8. The Late Period (Dynasties XXVI-XXXI *ca.* 663-332 BC). Nekau ("Necho") slew Josiah at Megiddo (2 Kings 23:29-30).

During this period, the Babylonians conquered Egypt. Nebuchadnezzar destroyed the Egyptians at Carchemish in 605 BC. When he took Jerusalem in 536 BC, Jews, including Jeremiah, fled to Egypt (Jer. 43:5-7).

Later in this period, the Persians defeated the Egyptians. Cambyses II, Cyrus' son, defeated Psamtik III at Pelusium in 525 BC and Egypt came under Persian rule.

9. The Ptolemaic Period (*ca.* 332-30 BC). In 333 BC, Alexander the Great defeated the Persians at Issus and was given Egypt. He built a capital at Alexandria. When he died, the Ptolemaic family took charge of Palestine and Egypt.

An ancient historian named Philo says a million Jews living in Egypt didn't know much Hebrew. So, the Hebrew Bible was translated into Greek (called the Septuagint). The Jews of

Alexandria were the first to use it. Later, it was read in synagogues throughout the Roman Empire.

10. The Roman Era (*ca.* 30 BC-AD 395). The Roman emperor Pompey captured Jerusalem in 63 BC. In an attempt to save Egypt, Cleopatra, a member of the Ptolemy family, courted the favor of Augustus Caesar and Mark Anthony. In 30 BC, when Caesar's fleet defeated hers at Actium, she committed suicide. From then on, Egypt was under Rome rule.

In 6/5 BC, Joseph and Mary fled to Egypt with the baby Jesus.

## ASSYRIA

The ancient land of Mesopotamia was composed of land between and on each side of the Tigris and Euphrates, stretching from the Persian Gulf to about 600 miles north (modern Iraq). The upper Tigris region was called Assyria. It took its name from its first capital, Asshur (Gen. 10:11). The history of Assyria can be divided into four parts.

1. Early History (2800-1900 BC). Uspia founded a settlement of Asshur *ca.* 2800 BC. Sargon of Agada (Akkad) ruled *ca.* 2350-2295 BC. Many believe he was the Nimrod of Genesis 10:8-12. He united the Mesopotamian region and controlled other areas as well. He was called the creator of the First World Empire.

2. Old Assyrian Period (1900-1300 BC). A strong family, under its head Shamshi-adad (*ca.* 1814-1782), controlled the area, even the distant city of Mari. After about 1750 BC, Assyria was at war with Babylon until about 1211 BC. These wars occupied

Assyria from when Israel was in Egypt and for many years of the Judges.

3. Middle Assyrian Period (1300-900 BC). Ashur-ballet I (*ca.* 1365-1330) reunited Assyria. Arik-den-ili (1319-1303) and Adad-nigari (1307-1275) regained territory to Carchemish. Shalmaneser I (1274-1245) established a new capital at Calah (Nimrod). Tiglath-Pileser I (1115-1097) was the first Assyrian King to march to the Mediterranean Sea. He pushed westward and northward, receiving tribute from Sidon and imposing taxes on the King of Hatti in northern Syria. In the meantime, David and Solomon extended their territory into southern Syria.

4. Neo-Assyrian Period (900-612 BC). After a period of decline, Ashurnasirpal II (885-860 BC) reestablished the empire. As his annals say, his army conquered a large area with ruthless cruelty. He is the one who introduced the most intense military training the world had ever known to that time. Troops were trained all year round instead of for only a few weeks. He also introduced systematic cruelty as a policy and used extreme torture on captives, cutting off their hands and ears, putting out their eyes, and piling them in heaps to die a slow, agonizing death. Some were flayed alive. Others were burned at the stake. Moreover, he and his successors took great pleasure in recording such cruelty in reliefs on the walls of their palaces.

Ashurnasirpal received tribute from Tyre, Sidon, and Byblos. That is as close as he got to Israel. His son, Shalmaneser III (859-824 BC), attempted to extend Assyrian rule into Palestine. In 853 BC, the Syrians, Irhuleni, and Adad-idri (Hadadezer, possibly

## Appendix

the Ben-Hadad II of 1 Kings 20), amassed a coalition at Karkara (Qarqar). According to Assyrian annals, "Ahab the Israelite" supplied 10,000 men and 2,000 chariots. This is the first reference to Israel in Assyrian records. Shalmaneser III lost the battle of Qarqar, which is not mentioned in the Bible, but several years later, he returned, marching all the way to Carmel on the Mediterranean Coast. In his Black Obelisk, now in the British Museum, "Jehu son of Amri" is pictured paying tribute. Shalmaneser conquered a large area during his king's reign but died amid a revolt that his son Shamshi-Adad V (823-811 BC) inherited.

Adad-nigari III (810-783 BC) once again made Assyria aggressive. In a stele, Adad-nigari lists tribute from "Joash of Samaria." Joash obtained Assyrian help against Syria (2 Kings 13, 25).

The next Assyrian ruler to reestablish control over outlying regions was Tiglath-Pileser III (*ca.* 745-727 BC). He conquered Babylon, where he was known as Pulu (See 2 Kings 15:19). Several years later, Tiglath-Pileser returned to Palestine. Second Kings 15:29 says, "In the days of Pekah King of Israel, Tiglath-Pileser King of Assyria came and took Ijon, Abel Beth Maachah, Janoah, Kedesh, Hazor, Gilead, and Galilee, all the land of Naphtali; and he carried them captive to Assyria."

Still later, when Syria and Israel (the Northern Kingdom) attacked Jerusalem, Ahaz, king of Judah, appealed to Tiglath-Pileser for help (2 King 16:5-8). Tiglath-Pileser then captured Damascus, the capital of Syria (2 Kings 16:9) and, according to his annals, he removed Pekah of Israel by assassination, set up

Hoshea as king, and annexed part of Israel (2 Kings 15:29-30). Tiglath-Pileser also extended the practice of transplanting captives to other lands and bringing in other captives to replace them (2 Kings 15:29).

Shalmaneser V (727-722 BC) succeeded his father, Tiglath-Pileser. The Assyrian eponym list states that he besieged Samaria for three years and the Babylonian chronicle tells how Shalmaneser "broke (the resistance) of the city of Samaria." At this point, the account and the Assyrian record are in agreement. Second Kings 17 says, "Shalmaneser King of Assyria" came against Hoshea (2 Kings 17:3) and "the King of Assyria" came against Hoshea (2 Kings 17:3) and "the King of Assyria" besieged Samaria for three years (2 Kings 17:5).

Sargon II (721-705 BC) was the next Assyrian ruler. In one of his inscriptions, he says, "The city Samaria I besieged and twenty-seven thousand two hundred and ninety people, inhabitants of it, I took away captive. Fifty chariots in it I seized, but the rest I allowed to retain their possessions." In his cylinder inscription, he calls himself "subjugator of the broad land of Beth-Omri" (that is, the descendants of Omri) and elsewhere "the conqueror of the city of Samaria and the whole land of Beth-Omri."

The book of 2 Kings does not name the king of Assyria, who finally conquered Samaria (see 2 Kings 17:6), though the context seems to suggest it was Shalmaneser. Perhaps Shalmaneser began the siege and Sargon II captured it after his death. Given the vagueness of the designations in 2 Kings 17, that could be the explanation of the account. Or maybe Shalmaneser and

## Appendix

Sargon II were co-rulers briefly before Shalmaneser died. Second Kings 18 says Shalmaneser besieged Samaria (2 Kings 18:9) and "they" took it (2 Kings 18:10). It has been suggested that Shalmaneser adopted Sargon and designed him as his successor (Unger). Sargon also continued the practice of Tiglath-Pileser of transplanting captives (2 Kings 17:6, 18:11-12). In 711 BC, Azuri, King of Ashdod, refused to pay the Assyria tribute. Sargon II sent the Assyrian general Tartan to Ashdod and he conquered it (Isa. 20:1).

Sennacherib (705-681 BC) succeeded his father Sargon II. In 701 BC, Sennacherib invaded Judah. Second Kings 18:13 says, "In the fourteenth year of King Hezekiah, Sennacherib King of Assyria came up against all the fortified cities of Judah and took them." In 1830, Colonel Taylor found one of the best-preserved extant Assyrian documents. It is a six-sided clay prism containing the final edition of Sennacherib's annals. This fourteen-and-a-half-inch high cylinder, the Taylor Cylinder, is now in the British Museum. It says: "As for Hezekiah the Jew, who did not submit to my yoke, forty-six of his strong-willed cities, as well as the small cities in their neighborhood, which were without number ... I besieged and took it."

At this point, Hezekiah paid tribute to Sennacherib at Lachish (2 Kings 18:14-16). The Taylor Cylinder mentions the tribute from Hezekiah and a wall relief found at Lachish pictures Sennacherib sitting on a throne receiving gifts. The inscription says, "Sennacherib, the King of the World, the king of Assyria, sat on his throne and the spoil of the city of Lachish marched before him."

Sennacherib besieged Jerusalem (2 Kings 18:17-19:34), which Hezekiah withstood. The Lord destroyed the Assyrian army (2 Kings 19:35-36). In the Taylor Cylinder (prism), Sennacherib says, "(Hezekiah) himself I shut up like a caged bird in Jerusalem, his royal city; the walls I fortified against him (and) whosoever came out of the gates of the city, I turned back." His statement proves he did not capture Jerusalem. He is silent about the cause of withdrawal. Like the Egyptians, the Assyrians reported only victories. The ancient historian Herodotus said mice devoured the Assyrian bowstrings and shield straps (ii. 141), which describes a plague.

Second Kings 19:37 says that as Sennacherib "was worshipping in the Temple of Nisroch his god...his sons Adrammelech and Sharezer struck him down with the sword." The Babylonian chronicle states that a son murdered him. He died on January 20, 681 BC.

Esarhaddon (681-669 BC), Sennacherib's youngest son, succeeded him (2 Kings 19:37).

Ashurbanipal (669-627 BC), Esarhaddon's son, succeeded his father. He was the last great Assyrian monarch. He took Manasseh prisoner to Babylon (2 Chron. 33:11).

After Ashurbanipal, several undistinguished kings ruled. Isaiah spoke to Hezekiah about the utter destruction of the Kings of Assyria (2 King 19:11-13; see also Isa. 37:11-12). In the meantime, Babylon was growing in power. In 626 BC, Nabopolassar, a Babylonian, defeated the Assyrians. In 612 BC, the combined forces of the Chaldeans, Medes and the Scythians

## Appendix

besieged Nineveh for about three months before it fell. Nebuchadnezzar, a Babylonian general at the time, defeated the final remnants of the Assyrian army (as well as the Egyptians) at Carchemish in 605 BC. Jeremiah speaks of this battle: "The word of the LORD which came to Jeremiah the prophet against the nations. Against Egypt. Concerning the army of Pharaoh Necho, king of Egypt, which was by the River Euphrates in Carchemish, and which Nebuchadnezzar king of Babylon defeated in the fourth year of Jehoiakim the son of Josiah, king of Judah" (Jer. 46:1-2).

This is one of the events in the Bible that can be verified outside that Bible. The Babylonian Chronicle records that Nebuchadnezzar, "the crown prince, mustered (the Babylon army) and took command of the Euphrates and crossed the river to go against the Egyptian army which lay in Carchemish ... fought with each other and the Egyptian army withdrew before him. He defeated and to non-existence beat them...."

Archaeology has excavated Carchemish and confirmed that the battle took place. After the Battle of Carchemish, Assyrian civilization then passed off the scene. By the way, the attack on Ashkelon is also recorded in Jeremiah (47:5-7) and in the Babylonian Chronicle.

## BABYLONIA

Ancient Mesopotamia was a land around the Tigris and Euphrates Rivers from the Persian Gulf to about 600 miles north (modern Iraq). The southern part of Mesopotamia has been called by several names, including the land of Shinar (Gen. 10:10), Babylon and the land of the Chaldeans (Jer. 24:5). Some of its major cities were Babel, Akkad (Agada), Ur, and Babylon.

Unlike the north (Assyria), a land of limestone hills and thick forests, the southern portion was flat and marshy, its soil rich and fertile. Consequently, the inhabitants of the south were more inclined to pursue peaceful agriculture. The Babylonians were not the warriors of their northern neighbors. The history of the southern region is as follows:

1. Early History (2800-*ca.* 1960 BC). During this period, dynasties of kings from several different cities ruled in their city and, in some cases, made themselves masters over other cities. Enmebaragesi established the first Dynasty of Kish. After that, Mesannepada took up the leading role at Ur, etc. Sargon founded a strong dynasty in a new city named Agada (Akkad). Some claim he was the Nimrod of Gen. 10:9-12. The third Dynasty of Ur was founded by Ur-Nammu, who built a ziggurat at Ur. During this Dynasty, Abraham was born and later left Ur.

2. Elamite and Amorite Invasions (*ca.* 1960-1830 BC). The Elamites sacked Ur. The Amorites from Mari conquered other cities.

3. Old Babylonian Period (*ca.* 1830-1550 BC). Rim-Sin (*ca.* 1823-1763 BC) of Larsa conquered Isin. Hammurabi (1792-1750 BC) ruled from Babylon. He defeated Rim-Sin and Kings from Elam, Mari, Eshnunna, etc. Hammurabi controlled a wide area. He became a ruler of the United Kingdom, extending from the Persian Gulf to the Habur (Khabur) River. The history of Babylon

## Appendix

is considered to begin with Hammurabi, the author of the famous Code of Hammurabi. During this period, the epic of creation called Emma Elish assumed the form used for the next thousand years. Excavations at Mari and Nuzi have shed much light on this period.

4. Kassite Invasions (*ca.* 1550-*ca.* 1169 BC). The Kassites (*ca.* 1550-1169 BC) conquered the land. Tukulti-Ninurta I, King of Assyria (1260-1232 BC) invaded Babylon and ruled for seven years. During this period, there was a dynasty of all native Babylonians at the city of Isin.

5. Assyrian Supremacy (*ca.* 1100-605 BC). Ashurnasirpal of Assyria (882-857 BC) conquered northern Babylon. His son, Shalmaneser III (857-822 BC), consolidated control. Tiglath-Pileser III (745-727 BC) took the title "King of Babylon," having claimed the throne under his native name of Pul(u) (2 Kings 15:14; 1 Chron. 5:26). His son Sargon II called himself "vice-regent of Babylon." His account of his destruction of Babylon in 709 BC has much in common with Isaiah 13:1-22. In 689 BC, Sennacherib sacked the city and burned it to the ground. Marduk-apla-iddina sought help for his resistance to the Assyrians, including overtures to Judah (2 Kings 20:12-19; Isa. 39), but he fled into exile. The sacking of Babylon by the Assyrians in 692 BC is the background of Isaiah's prophecies against Babylon (Isa. 14:39; 43:14). The Assyrian King Esarhaddon had a conciliatory policy toward Babylon.

6. Neo-Babylonia (Chaldean Empire, *ca.* 605-539 BC). In 625 BC, Nabopolassar founded the Neo-Babylonian or Chaldean

Empire. With the help of the Medes, the Assyrians were driven back until, in August of 612 BC, Nineveh fell.

The greatest king in Babylon's history was Nebuchadnezzar, Nabopolassar's son. In 605 BC, he defeated the Egyptians at Carchemish. Then, according to Josephus, he "conquered the whole of Syro-Palestine" (*Antiquities*. x. 6.86; see 2 Kings 24:7.). When Nabopolassar died, Nebuchadnezzar succeeded his father to the throne (Sept. 6, 605 BC). On March 16, 597 BC, he conquered Jerusalem, took Jehoiachin to Babylon, and made Mattaniah king (2 Kings 24:8-17; Nebuchadnezzar changed Mattaniah's name to Zedekiah). Babylonian tablets confirm Jehoiachin's captivity. When Zedekiah rebelled (2 Kings 24:20), Jerusalem was attacked again and sacked (2 Kings 25:1-21). The Babylonians later invaded Egypt (Jer. 4:6).

Nebuchadnezzar is quoted in Daniel as saying, "Is not this great Babylon that I have built" (Dan. 4:30). Indeed, he did. The Euphrates River ran through the city. The ancient historian Herodotus described the city as overwhelming in magnitude, including the rebuilt ziggurat that was eight stages high and the Hanging Gardens, which the Greeks called one of the Seven Wonders of the World.

Nebuchadnezzar was succeeded by Amel-Marduk (562-560 BC), Evil-Merodach of 2 Kings 24:27-30 and Jeremiah 52:31-34. Then followed Neriglissar (560-556 BC), Labashi-Marduk (556 BC), and Nabonidus (556-539 BC).

Against all the odds, the Persians conquered Babylon. A double wall protected Babylon. The inner wall was 21 feet thick,

## Appendix

with large towers rising 30-60 feet high at intervals of about 60 feet. It has been estimated that there were at least a hundred of these. Twenty-three feet away was the outer wall, which was 12 feet thick. Still further outside, another 65 feet, was a moat. According to two ancient historians, Herodotus and Xenophon, the Persians entered the city of Babylon by diverting the Euphrates River, which flowed under the city wall and through the city.

The conquering army found the people in a drunken festival. Daniel records what happened that night, describing Belshazzar and others drinking wine from the sacred vessels his father, Nebuchadnezzar, took from the Temple in Jerusalem. It was Belshazzar who saw God's handwriting of judgment on the wall of the banquet hall. Daniel concludes by saying, "That very night Belshazzar, king of the Chaldeans, was slain" (Dan. 5:30). Nabonidus' son and co-regent Belshazzar was killed on October 12, 539 BC.

Babylon was annexed to Persia and lost its independence.

## PERSIA

East of the Tigris River is a vast plateau that extends to the Indus River (on the other side of which is India). This plateau is bordered on the west by the Zagros Mountains. The Caspian Sea is on the north and the Persian Gulf lies to the south. This large area is known as ancient Persia (modern Iran). Before about 1000 BC, the southwest portion was occupied by the Elamites. The Medes and the Persians arrived around 1000 BC.

1. The Medes. Repeated attacks by the Assyrians and others forced the Medes to unite. Their capital was Ecbatana. In alliance with the Medes, the Babylonians sacked Nineveh in 612 BC. They shared the spoils equally. The granddaughter of a Medean King married Nebuchadnezzar. It was for her (Amytis) that the Hanging Gardens of Babylon were built.

2. The Persians. The founder of the Persian Empire was Cyrus II, the Great (559-530 BC). He conquered the Medes and took Ecbatana. He grew greater and greater until the supremacy of Persia was established. His capital was Pasargadae. He is the one who issued the decree restoring the Jews to their homeland (Ezra 1:1-3; 2 Chron. 36:22). He was buried in a tomb at Pasargadae, which is still extant.

Cambyses II (529-522 BC), Cyrus' son, succeeded him. He conquered Egypt.

Darius I (522-486 BC) was the next king. He built a new place at Susa (521 BC) and an entirely new capital was founded at Persepolis (518 BC). Under him, the Persian Empire reached the heights of its power and glory, from Egypt to India.

Darius' son, Xerxes (486-465 BC) succeeded his father. Xerxes is the Ahasuerus of the Book of Esther.

Artaxerxes I ("Longimanus") (465-423) followed Xerxes. Ezra went to Jerusalem in the seventh year of this king (Ezra 7:1-8). Nehemiah was his cupbearer (Neh. 2:1).

The other Persian kings were Darius II (423-404 BC), Artaxerxes II Mnemon (404-359 BC), Artaxerxes III Ochus (359-338 B.C), Artaxerxes III (338-335 BC), and Darius III (335-331

*Appendix*

BC) who was the King when the declining empire fell to Alexander the Great.

## ROME

Rome, the city-state that became an empire, is located on the Tiber River in the Italian peninsula, about seventeen miles from the Mediterranean Sea. The origin of the city is more mythological than historical. According to Cicero, Rome takes its name from its founder, Romulus. The myth is that Romulus was the son of Mars.

1. The Monarchy (753-509 BC). The traditional date of the founding of Rome is 753 BC. Rome was governed by kings and a consul until *ca.* 509 BC.

2. The Republic (509-27 BC). In 509 BC, a revolt resulted in the establishment of a Republic. The kingly office was abolished and consuls governed. Rome increased steadily in power and influence. In 338 BC, Rome dissolved the Latin League and controlled central Italy. During the Punic Wars (264-146 BC), Carthage was defeated (202 BC) and Corinth was destroyed (146 BC). Pompeius Magnus conquered Palestine in 63 BC.

From 63 to 31 BC, there was a civil war. The first Triumvirate, consisting of Julius Caesar, Pompeius Magnus ("Pompey the Great") and Marcus Crassus, was formed to rule the state in 60 BC (Caesar's famous Gallic Wars took place between 58-51 BC). In 44 BC, the struggle for power between Pompey and Julius Caesar ended with the assassination of Caesar. The second Triumvirate, consisting of Octavian, Mark Antony, and Marcus Aemilius

Lepidus, was formed in 43 BC. This Triumvirate conquered the forces under Brutus and Cassius at Philippi in 42 BC. As a result of the Battle of Actium in 31 BC, Octavian, later called Augustus, became the sole ruler. The territory of the Roman Empire at the time of Augustus extended from the Atlantic (Spain) to the Euphrates, from the Black Sea to the Cataracts of the Nile, and the population was estimated at eighty-five million.

3. The Empire. In a sense, Julius Caesar (100-44 BC) was the founder of the Empire. The Triumvirate and the consul officially ruled, but by 49 BC, Caesar secured supreme power. Although he was not an emperor, when he died on the Ides of March 44 BC, he was both chief of the senate and high priest (Latin *pontifex maximus*). Octavian (Gaius Julius Caesar Augustus, 63 BC- AD 14) was the official founder of the Empire. He succeeded Julius Caesar. Octavian defeated Mark Antony and Cleopatra of Egypt at Actium on September 2, 31 BC. The formal beginning of the Roman Empire occurred on January 16, 27 BC, with the bestowal of the title Augustus on Octavian. Though there was a show of republican government, Augustus Caesar ruled as a virtual absolute monarch (a "military monarch"). He had complete control of the legislature, the administration and the army. During his reign, Jesus was born. Under Tiberius (AD 14-37), John the Baptist and Jesus conducted their ministries. Caligula (AD 37-41) was the next of the Julian Emperors. Paul conducted missionary journeys when Claudius (AD 41-54) reigned. Under Nero (AD 54-68), Rome was burned, Christians were persecuted and Paul and Peter were martyred.

## Appendix

Only a few Roman cities are mentioned in the New Testament, namely, Puteoli (Acts 28:13), Appii Forum (Acts 28:15), Three Inns (Acts 28:15), and, of course, Rome. While traveling from Puteoli to Rome, Paul walked the Appian Way, the oldest and most famous of the Roman roads. Parts of it can still be seen today. Paul may have been arraigned before Nero in the Forum, the ruins of which are in Rome today. After the famous Roman fire destroyed his palace in AD 64, Nero built a massive new palace complex, including parks and a lake. Eighty-eight rooms of Nero's palace on Oppian Hill have been found and cleared. Paul was probably imprisoned in the Mamertine Prison, near the west end of the Roman Forum. Some of its ruins still exist. There is a persistent tradition that during Nero's persecution, Peter was buried in what is now the area of the Vatican. The Roman Catholic Church claims that His body is buried under the altar of Saint Peter's Basilica in the Vatican area. Excavations conducted from 1940 to 1949 and again in 1953 found bones which the Roman Catholic Church claims are those of Peter, though others are not so certain.

When Nero died, the struggle for power resulted in the beginning of the Flavian line. Vespasian (AD 69-79) was the Roman emperor when Jerusalem revolted and was destroyed by his son Titus (AD 70). Titus only ruled for two years (AD 79-81); he died young. Between AD 72 and 80, long after Peter and Paul were martyred at Rome, Vespasian and Titus built the Coliseum, a massive structure with rising tiers of seats circling an open space. In AD 79, Mount Vesuvius erupted, burying Pompeii in 19 to 23 feet of volcanic ash. It is estimated that of a population of twenty thousand, about two thousand perished.

Domitian (Titus Flavius Domitianus) (AD 88-96) took the title "Lord and God" and persecuted Christians. John was exiled to the Isle of Patmos, where he wrote the book of Revelation.

Hadrian (AD 117-133) rebuilt Jerusalem as a pagan city called Aelia Capitoline.

Diocletian (AD 284-303) was the greatest persecutor of Christians.

Constantine (AD 312-327) made Christianity a legal religion.

Rome was defeated in AD 476.

## About The Author

G. Michael Cocoris is a gifted communicator. He can make even complicated subjects simple, clear, and practical. His breadth of experience has allowed him to relate to a wide range of audiences.

Michael received a Bachelor of Arts degree from Tennessee Temple University, a Master of Theology degree from Dallas Seminary, and a Doctorate of Divinity from Biola University. He traveled the United States for over a dozen years as a speaker. He has also been a seminary professor, visiting lecturer, and world traveler, including hosting tours to Israel and China.

Michael has pastored three churches, including a rural church when he was in seminary, an urban church, the historic Church of the Open Door, first in downtown Los Angeles and later in Glendora, California, and a suburban church, the Lindley Church in Tarzana California, a suburb of Los Angeles. While at the Church of Open Door, he had a daily radio broadcast.

Michael has written numerous magazine articles, mainly for *Biblical Research Monthly*. He has authored a number of books, including *Seventy Years on Hope Street, A History of the Church of the Open Door*; *How To Live A Biblical Spiritual Life, Clarifying the Confusion*; *Repentance, The Most Misunderstood Word in the Bible*; *Evangelism: A Biblical Approach*; *The Salvation Controversy*; *Lordship Salvation: Is It Biblical?*; *The Books of the Bible, the Subject, Structure, Situation, and Significant Verses of Each Book*; *Psalms, A Song for Every Situation, Each Summarized on One Page*; and *Counseling Theories, A Biblical Evaluation*. In addition, he was a contributor to The *NKJV Study Bible* and *Nelson's New Illustrated Bible Commentary*.

Michael is the pastor of the Lindley Church in Tarzana, California. He and his wife, Patricia, live in Santa Monica, California.

www.ingramcontent.com/pod-product-compliance
Lightning Source LLC
Chambersburg PA
CBHW070104080526
44586CB00013B/1178